Pitkin County Library

120 North Mill Street
Aspen, Colorado 81611
(970) 429-1900

WITHDRAWN

263.2 B918
Buchanan, Mark (Mark Aldham) 17.99
The rest of God : restoring
your soul by restoring
Sabbath

DATE DUE

GAYLORD PRINTED IN U.S.A.

Praise for *The Rest of God* and Mark Buchanan

"Buchanan campaigns persuasively for readers to revive the Sabbath as a refuge from our pervasive and spiritually destructive culture of busyness. His prose is fresh and immediate, earnest and self-effacing at the same time."

–*Publishers Weekly*

"For too long now debates over how to observe the Lord's Day have lacked two things: spirit and imagination. Mark Buchanan restores both in this delightfully inspiring book. Beginning with the human being's need for rest, working through the problem of mindset and time usage, and focusing our perspective on God and His good plan for our lives, Mark takes us on a tour de force of glorious Sabbath-keeping that can bring God's rest not only to our Sundays, but to every day of our lives."

–Charles Colson
Founder and Chairman
Prison Fellowship

"With the easiness of long intimacy and a very deft hand, Buchanan here braids together into one gracious and sustaining strand the beauty of the Sabbath, the wisdom of its keeping, and the generosity of God in gifting us with it. These pages are not just a blessing, they are a psalm that cries out to be joyfully engaged."

–Phyllis Tickle
Religion Editor (ret.) *Publishers Weekly*
and compiler of *The Divine Hours*

"It seems very unsabbath-like to describe a book about Sabbath with the adverb "urgently"—but we urgently need this book. Mark Buchanan shows us that our business is killing us—killing us—and that Sabbath is our best cure, our best path for rest and reverence and discipleship."

–Lauren Winner
Best-selling author of *Girl Meets* God and *Mudhouse Sabbath*

"Mark Buchanan's writing always leaves me moved, stimulated, and convicted. I find myself mulling it over days later and wishing for more."

–Philip Yancey
Best-selling author

"Buchanan's book hits the mark with finely turned phrases that make reading this a joy"

–*Publishers Weekly* (review of *Things Unseen*)

"Buchanan masterfully wields a pen, like Edgar Martinez, a baseball bat. Buchanan brings a background in literature and writing into his life as a pastor in British Columbia. To his mix of literature and theology, he also brings an eye for personality, a nose for story, and the heart of a shepherd. The combination sizzles."

– *Moody* magazine

Mark Buchanan holds familiar things up to the light and rediscovers for us the depths and the mystery of what it means to be alive. In his hands the concept of Sabbath is transformed from an archaic inconvenient humbug into a life-giving, life-restoring gift we simply cannot afford to ignore. Mark invites us to stop and rediscover the rest of God, and gives us permission to enjoy it.

–John Ellis, Lead vocalist, Tree63

A craftsman skilled with words, Mark Buchanan has written a penetrating book with an easy contemplative tone. This is enjoyable reading about something precious most of us have lost, and some of us have never known. I needed to sit back, relax and savor this heart-moving, thought-provoking book. I suspect you do, too.

–Randy Alcorn, Best-selling author

THE REST OF GOD

Restoring Your Soul by Restoring Sabbath

Mark Buchanan

W Publishing Group
A Division of Thomas Nelson Publishers
Since 1798
www.wpublishinggroup.com

THE REST OF GOD

Copyright © 2006 Mark Buchanan

All rights reserved. No portion of this book may be reproduced, stored in a retrieval system, or transmitted in any form or by any means—electronic, mechanical, photocopy, recording, or any other—except for brief quotations in printed reviews, without the prior written permission of the publisher.

Published by W Publishing Group, a Division of Thomas Nelson, Inc., P.O. Box 141000, Nashville, Tennessee 37214.

W Publishing Group books may be purchased in bulk for educational, business, fund-raising, or sales promotional use. For information, please e-mail SpecialMarkets@ThomasNelson.com.

All Scripture quotations, unless otherwise indicated, are taken from The Holy Bible, New International Version (NIV). Copyright © 1973, 1978, 1984. International Bible Society. Used by permission of Zondervan Bible Publishers.

Other Scripture references are from the following sources:
The New American Standard Bible (NASB), © 1960, 1977, 1995 by the Lockman Foundation.

The Message (MSG), copyright © 1993. Used by permission of NavPress Publishing Group.

The New King James Version (NKJV). Copyright © 1979, 1980, 1982 by Thomas Nelson, Inc. Used by permission. All rights reserved.

Editorial Staff: Holly Halverson, Sue Ann Jones, Lauren Weller, Deborah Wiseman
Page Design: Lori Lynch, Book and Graphic Design, Nashville, TN

Published in association with the literary agency of Ann Spangler and Company, 1420 Pontiac Road SE, Grand Rapids, MI 49506.

Library of Congress Cataloging-in-Publication Data

Buchanan, Mark (Mark Aldham)
The rest of God : restoring your soul by restoring Sabbath / Mark Buchanan.
p. cm.
ISBN 0-8499-1848-0
263.2
BUC
2.07
1. Rest—Religious aspects—Christianity. 2. Sabbath. I. Title.
BV4597.55.B83 2005
263'.2—dc22 2005010012

Printed in the United States of America
06 07 08 09 10 QW 9 8 7 6 5 4 3 2 1

I dedicate this book to my three children:

Adam,

Sarah,

Nicola.

Through you I find the rest of God.

> I will always remind you of these things, even though you know them and are firmly established in the truth you now have. I think it is right to refresh your memory as long as I live in the tent of this body, because I know that I will soon put it aside, as our Lord Jesus Christ has made clear to me. And I will make every effort to see that after my departure you will alwas be able to remember these things. (2 Peter 1:12–15)

These verses define what I'm about, as both a writer and a speaker; the ministry of reminding—of restating truth we alreaady know. I do this always, and I will do it as long as I'm around, so that even after I've departed, the memory of truth will live on. I hope what I write is fresh, but there is nothing original. It's all just a reminder.

–Mark Buchanan

I don't know exactly what a prayer is.
I do know how to pay attention, how to fall down
into the grass, how to kneel down in the grass,
how to be idle and blessed, how to stroll through the fields,
which is what I have been doing all day.
Tell me, what else should I have done?

—Mary Oliver

Be still, and know that I am God.

—Psalm 46:10

CONTENTS

Acknowledgments

This book is the work of many hands. I wrote it myself, true, in an almost monastic solitude. But I was never quite alone: so many others, the living and the dead, by providence or design, helped shape what you hold now. This page is my modest—stingy, really—attempt to thank a few.

Joy Brewster. Lois Mitchell. Allan Kinnee. You each took time to read an early (and messy) draft and to make wise and helpful comments. This book is different because of you: better, I think. If it is, thank you. If it's not, thanks a lot—I mean, it's not your fault. Thank you for your encouragement and honesty.

Allan Kinnee (again) and Rob Filgate: I'm grateful for our friendship, even if you both make terrible squash partners. But love covers over a multitude of sins.

Greg Daniel. To you I owe the initial inspiration for this book, and your discerning comments along the way helped make it stronger and clearer. Your challenge to write about Sabbath proved personally subversive and redemptive. I hope reading this book proves so for others.

Kate Etue and Holly Halverson: your keen eyes and sharp scalpel in editing redeemed me, many times, from my own grammatical clumsiness.

Ann Spangler. You're not only a great agent, but a good friend. I treasure our Sabbath times together.

My church, New Life Community Baptist. You get more and more peculiar every year, and it is such an honor to take Sabbath with you. I am sorry I have not always shown you the rest of God, but I'm learning.

My family. You keep drawing me back to this deep truth: *Not by strength, nor by might, but by my Spirit, says the Lord.* I love you.

My God. Thank you for life and life abundant. All glory is yours.

CATNAP: *An Invitation to Stop*

My parents loved cats. You should have seen them in their heyday, the house a colony of fur and the furniture like so many lint brushes, thickly thatched with cat hair. And, of course, the cats themselves, cats everywhere: sassy, sauntering, shedding, mewling, purring, hissing, lounging, lunging. The sight of some wiry poodle or jowly hound made their backs arch and quill with hackles, their tails go ramrod straight and bristle out like chimney brooms. The sight of a bird pecking seed awakened in them ancient bloodthirst, quickened near-dormant instincts, and suddenly that drowsy, half-oblivious cat was crouched low, eyes sharp as sickles, all stealth and appetite.

My parents had Siamese, devious and haughty and aloof, their coats glistening smooth as a baby seal's. They had Himalayans, foolish and dumbfounded and clumsy, their hair disheveled and shocked out like Einstein's. They had sleek, charming tabbies; languid and sullen Persians; surly, bony whatchamacallits. They had Pooh Bear, a hapless, witless furball and a coward of legendary proportions. That cat suffered warlike trauma from the taunting—I'm not making this up—of the neighborhood toms. Many nights Pooh Bear woke us all with his desperate caterwauling, treed again by the neighborhood bullies—a gang of scrawny and not-too-bright felines whose power to create terror clearly exceeded their power to deliver on it. But their bluff worked on our cat. Each encounter made Pooh a bit more skittish, easily spooked by thunderclap or wind gust.

A low point in my childhood was the day Pooh Bear came home with his whiskers sheared to stubs. How this happened I'll never know. But because I didn't like the cat—I thought him timid and spoiled—I was blamed. To this day, my family still accuses me of cutting his whiskers, and the only thing that's ever kept me from mounting a more vigorous self-defense is that, though I never touched him, I'd thought of worse things I might do to him, and that's its own kind of fault.

I ended up a dog lover.

But I remember with affection one thing about all those cats. Despite their widely varied personalities—as different as people, as the people you work with or live with—they had one thing in common: they all liked to sleep in the patches of sunlight that fell, bright and jut-angled, through our front window in the late afternoon of a winter's day. Where we lived the winters were impossibly cold. You grew afraid that things—houses, cars, body parts, the ground itself—might break from sheer brittleness, break into a million glassy splinters. There were weeks on end when to send your cat outside was a sure death sentence, an act of cruelty so dastardly even the hard of heart would stay their hands from committing it.

I wouldn't even send Pooh Bear out into that.

So we kept the cats in and made little boxes mounded with cat litter for them to do their business, fed them more food in a day than they could burn up in a week, and watched them grow waddling fat.

And we watched them sleep. As the afternoon pushed headlong into night, the sun, clipping swift across an icy sky, tipped westward and thrust its fingers into our living room. Then the cats emerged from wherever else they had been in the house to curl up or sprawl out in the warm pools of light that scattered across furniture and floor. They lay in utter contentment, with almost boneless stillness, spread out like so many jugs and basins placed under a prairie sky to catch rainwater after drought. The impression I got was that those cats were emptying themselves and filling themselves all at once. It was not a long sleep. It was a catnap. This was winter, remember, and we lived at the edge of the earth, where night swallowed day quick and whole. But in that brief spell, that sunlight was oasis, heavenboon, pure grace.

I learned to join them, the cats in their cradles of sunlight. I curled up or sprawled out beside them and catnapped too. It had a unique power to replenish. Fifteen, twenty minutes later, a shadow like a cool, dry hand edged up my flesh and nudged me awake. I stirred, sat up, and went about the rest of my day, freshly aware.

That image comes to mind when I think of Sabbath: a patch of sunlight falling through a window on a winter's day. It's a small yet ample chunk of space, a narrow yet full segment of time. In it, you can lie down and rest. From it, you can rise up and go—stronger, lighter, ready to work again with vigor and a clear mind. It is room enough, time enough, in which to relinquish all encumbrances, to act as though their existence has nothing whatsoever to do with your own. It is an invitation, at one and the same time, to empty yourself and fill yourself.

In the book of Acts, Philip the evangelist meets a nobleman from Ethiopia. He's the treasurer for Ethiopia's queen, an important man on important business. He's a man in such a hurry that he does his reading while racing along on his chariot, like someone checking his Palm Pilot for e-mails between phone calls and strategy meetings.

The Spirit prompts Philip to come alongside him. It is one of God's strange works of choreography: the Ethiopian at that very moment is reading something from Isaiah, something that stirs in him wonder and hunger. It gives him a taste of something else, something more, and leaves him dissatisfied with life as he knows it. Philip arrives at just such a time as this and introduces him to Jesus.

As they travel, they come to a pool of water. "Look, here is water," the Ethiopian says to Philip. "Why shouldn't I be baptized?"

There's no reason why he shouldn't. So the Ethiopian orders the driver to stop. They pile out of the chariot, go down to the water, and Philip baptizes him.

That's akin to what I'm up to here. I believe God has choreographed this moment, that the Spirit has prompted it, and that I'm called to come alongside you as you race to whatever important thing you have to do next. Maybe you're even reading this book as you go—on a plane, on a train, in a bus, on a boat. Going somewhere, going fast.

I believe the Spirit has brought us into each other's company for just such a time as this, that together we might discover Jesus in the midst of our busyness.

And look! Here's a patch of sunlight.

Why shouldn't you stop and rest?

Starting to Stop

The world is not dying for another book.

But it is dying for the rest of God.

I certainly was. I became a Sabbath-keeper the hard way: either that, or die. Not die literally—at least, I don't think so—but die in other ways. It happened subtly, over time; but I noticed at some point that the harder I worked, the less I accomplished. I was often a whirligig of motion. My days were intricately fitted together like the old game of Mousetrap, every piece precariously connected to every other, the whole thing needing to work together for it to work at all.

But there was little joy, and stunted fruit.

To justify myself, I'd tell others I was gripped by a magnificent obsession. I was purpose-driven, I said, or words like that. It may have begun that way. It wasn't that way any longer. Often I was just obsessed, merely driven, no magnificence or purposefulness about it. I once went forty days—an ominously biblical number, that—without taking a single day off.

And was proud of it.

But things weren't right. Though my work often consumed me, I was losing my pleasure in it—and, for that matter, in many other things besides—and losing, too, my effectiveness in it. And here's a secret: for all my busyness, I was increasingly slothful. I could wile away hours at a time in a masquerade of working, a pantomime of toil—fiddling about on the computer, leafing through old magazines, chatting up people in the hallways. But I was squandering time, not redeeming it. And whenever I stepped out for a vacation, I did just that: vacated, evacuated, spilled myself empty. I folded in on myself like a tent suddenly bereft of stakes and ropes and poles, clapped hard by the wind. The air went out of me.

The inmost places suffered most. I was losing perspective. Fissures in my character worked themselves here and there into cracks. Some widened into ruptures. I grew easily irritable, paranoid, bitter, self-righteous, gloomy. I was often argumentative: I preferred rightness to intimacy. I avoided and I withdrew. I had a few people I confided in, but few friends. I didn't understand friendship. I had a habit of turning people, good people who genuinely cared for me, into extensions of myself: still water for me to gaze at the way Narcissus did, dark caves for me to boom my voice into and bask in the echoes. I didn't let anyone get too near.

And then I came to my senses. I wish I could say this happened in one blazing, dazzling vision—a voice from heaven, a light that blinded and wounded and healed—but it didn't. It was more a slow dawning. I didn't lose my marriage, or family, or ministry, or health. I didn't wallow in pig muck, scavenging for husks and rinds. But it became clear that if I continued in the way I was heading, I was going to do lasting damage. And it became obvious that the pace and scale of my striving were paying diminishing returns. My drivenness was doing no one any favors. I couldn't keep it up and had no good excuse to try.

I learned to keep Sabbath in the crucible of breaking it.

God made us from dust. We're never too far from our origins. The apostle Paul says we're only clay pots—dust mixed with water, passed through fire. Hard, yes, but brittle too. Knowing this, God gave us the gift of Sabbath—not just as a day, but as an orientation, a way of seeing and knowing. Sabbath-keeping is a form of mending. It's mortar in the joints. Keep Sabbath, or else break too easily, and oversoon. Keep it, otherwise our dustiness consumes us, becomes us, and we end up able to hold exactly nothing.

In a culture where busyness is a fetish and stillness is laziness, rest is sloth. But without rest, we miss the rest of God: the rest he invites us to enter more fully so that we might know him more deeply. "Be still, and know that I am God." Some knowing is never pursued, only received. And for that, you need to be still.

Sabbath is both a day and an attitude to nurture such stillness. It is both time on a calendar and a disposition of the heart. It is a day we enter, but just as much a way we see. Sabbath imparts the rest of God—actual physical, mental, spiritual rest, but also the *rest* of God—the things of God's nature and presence we miss in our busyness.

You might have grown up legalistic about Sabbath—your principal memory of it is of stiff collars chafing at the neck and a vast, stern silence that settled on the house like a grief. I hope to invite you out of the rigidity and gloom that mark the day for you.

You might have grown up indifferent about Sabbath—Sabbath to you is a musty, creaky thing about which only ancient rabbis and old German Mennonites bother. I hope to awaken in you wonder and expectancy about it. I'm going to make a bold assumption and guess that this description fits you closer than the other: that you tend to see Sabbath, even if you grew up under legalism, as something archaic and arcane. Something from which you're exempt. Something that, like bloomers and corsets and top hats, went out of style long ago and is not likely to make a comeback soon.

I hope to convince you otherwise: that Sabbath, in the long run, is as essential to your well-being as food and water, and as good as a wood fire on a cold day.

I am going to be bold enough to assume one more thing: that you are just plain tired, and often overwhelmed—such that even Sabbath seems just one more thing to do. I hope to tune your ears to better hear, and gladly accept, Jesus's invitation: "Come to Me, all who are weary and heavy-laden, and I will give you rest" (Matt. 11:28 NASB).

One thing I've already hinted but need to make explicit: when I use the word *Sabbath,* I mean two things. I mean a day, the seventh day in particular. For Jewish people, that day is sundown Friday to sundown Saturday. For most Christians, it has traditionally been Sunday, however you reckon it, evening to evening or daybreak to daybreak or midnight to midnight. I want to convince you, in part, that setting apart an entire day, one out of seven, for feasting and resting and worship and play is a gift and not a burden, and neglecting the gift too long will make your soul, like soil never left fallow, hard and dry and spent.

But when I say *Sabbath,* I also mean an attitude. It is a perspective, an orientation. I mean a Sabbath heart, not just a Sabbath day. A Sabbath heart is restful even in the midst of unrest and upheaval. It is attentive to the presence of God and others even in the welter of much coming and going, rising and falling. It is still and knows God even when mountains fall into the sea.

You will never enter the Sabbath day without a Sabbath heart. In this book, I sometimes use the word *Sabbath* to refer to both, and sometimes to one or the other. But always my assumption is that both are needed and that each reinforces the other.

"Of course!" the poet Mary Oliver exclaims in one of her earthy, ethereal poems. "The path to heaven / doesn't lie down in flat miles. / It's in the imagination / with which you perceive / this world, / and the gestures / with which you honor it."[1]

The imagination with which you perceive this world. In many ways, this book is a call to your imagination, an attempt to awaken in you fresh ways of perceiving this world, fresh ways of understanding both your place and God's presence within it. Any deep change in how we live begins with a deep change in how we think. The biblical word for this is *repentance*—in Greek, *metanoia*, a change of mind. Repentance is a ruthless dismantling of old ways of seeing and thinking, and then a diligent and vigilant building of new ones.

Change begins with fresh eyes, in other words. It begins with an awakened imagination. You turn away, stubbornly and without apology, from that which formerly entranced you, and you turn toward that which once you avoided. You start to see what God sees, and as God sees it. But that takes more than will. It also takes imagination.

According to the apostle Paul, sin's fortress is your mind: the ultimate consequence of evil behavior, he says, is that it makes us "enemies in [our] minds" toward God (Col. 1:21). So God in Christ, and Christ through the Holy Spirit, is seeking to change our minds. All who are in Christ, Paul declares, are new creations being transformed "by the renewing of your mind," being "made new in the attitude of your minds" (Rom. 12:2; Eph. 4:23). We have exclusive access to the "mind of Christ" (1 Cor. 2:16). The apostle Peter, likewise, tells us that God has revealed to us his salvation—a salvation the prophets foretold but never beheld, which angels "long to look into" but for some reason have been denied the privilege (1 Pet. 1:12). The gift has come to us alone.

Peter urges this response: "Therefore, prepare your minds for action" (1 Pet. 1:13).

When salvation comes, change your mind. Reshape and fill fresh the imagination with which you perceive the world.

The movie *A Beautiful Mind* is about the brilliant mathematician John Nash, who, despite his schizophrenia, won the Nobel prize in 1994 for his original contribution to mathematics. John inhabits a world that doesn't actually exist: his closest friend, his friend's lovely niece, the CIA director who employs him in dangerous and clandestine operations—all are figments of his broken mind. When John is first diagnosed with the disease, he is treated with medication. This banishes his delusions but also stifles his personality: he becomes a hollow man, a mechanism. Gradually, through his wife's immense patience, fortitude, and sacrifice, John learns to live with his disease untreated. Except for one thing: he disciplines himself to no longer heed the people and the voices that his mind invents. Though even in his old age they appear to him as real as himself—flesh-and-blood people, with histories and personalities and needs and expectations, clamoring for his attention and affection and obedience—he refuses to listen. He defies them. He ignores them. He walks past them.

He changes his mind.

It's not a bad image for repentance: the voices that once held sway over us, that loomed so large and boomed so loud they defined reality, we now defy or ignore. We pay them heed no longer, though they try with all their might to resume their former dominance. We keep walking past them.

We change our minds.

This change of mind is meant to touch every aspect of how we see and think. And, God being my helper, that's what I'm trying to do in this book: to help us think differently about time and eternity, rest and work, food and play—to change and renew our minds about such things (of course, I can do nothing apart from Christ and the Spirit). Unless he illumines and empowers these words—shapes them into a sword that becomes companion to the sword of his own Word—they remain cold and inert as scrap metal, able to penetrate or separate nothing.

But this must be practical too. We need to change our minds, yes, but we also need to change our ways. And for this we require *practices* to embody and rehearse our change of mind. The physical is a handmaiden to the spiritual, but a necessary one, without practices—without *gestures with which to honor* fresh ways of perceiving—any change of mind will be superficial, artificial, short-lived. We might attain a genuinely new thought, but without some way of putting it into practice, the thought gets stuck in abstractions, lost in forgetting.

Good practices are both catalysts and incubators for new

thoughts, they initiate them, and they nurture them. But they do even more: *they make real our change of mind.* It's like marriage. When I married my wife, Cheryl, I had to change my mind about who I was. I was no longer a bachelor. My habits of thought had, for more than twenty years, taken shape around the fact of my singleness. I had bachelor attitudes about how to spend time and money, about the ideal color to paint a bedroom, about the best car to drive, about other women. It all had to go through a dramatic shift, in some cases a complete about-face, when I took vows (actually, the change began a long time prior to that, and continues lifelong). I had to—have to—change my mind.

But if *I changed only my mind and never changed my behavior,* I doubt I'd still be married. I have needed, at every turn, practices that embody and rehearse—*that make real*—my change of mind.

Zacchaeus is a good example of how this works. Zacchaeus was Jericho's runtish tax collector who went out on a limb for Jesus: he shimmied up the trunk of a sycamore tree, scrambled out on its branches, and perched there baboonlike just to catch a glimpse of Jesus. Jesus liked him, though no one else in town apparently did. Jesus asked him to get down from that tree immediately: "I want to come to your house today."

"Look, Lord!" Zacchaeus says in response. "Here and now I give half of my possessions to the poor, and if I have cheated anybody out of anything, I will pay back four times the amount" (Luke 19:8). Zacchaeus meets Jesus and changes his mind, but straight on the heels of that, he changes his ways. He embraces a practice that embodies and rehearses his new way of seeing. Jesus's comment on the matter is telling: "Today salvation has come to this house" (Luke 19:9). When salvation comes to your house, first you think differently, then you act differently. First you shift *the imagination with which you perceive this world,* and then you enact *gestures with which you honor it.*

Throughout this book, as I try to change your mind about Sabbath,

I will also suggest some *gestures with which to honor it.* These suggested practices I have placed at the end of each chapter and under a single heading: "Sabbath Liturgy."

Liturgy. I chose that word with care.

I was converted within a Low Church tradition, where the building's walls are stark, the music simple, the prayers clumsy and direct, made up as you pray them. I have only ever belonged to that tradition. And so early on I picked up the tradition's historic suspicion of High Church, where God is approached through a sometimes elaborate system of symbol and ritual—robes and candles and prayer books and lectionaries—and almost everything is scripted.

That scripting is liturgy.

Yet over time I began to realize that the Low Church is just as bound by liturgy as any church, and maybe more so because we think we're not. The Low Church enshrines—*makes a liturgy of*—austerity, spontaneity, informality. And we have our unwritten but nonetheless rigorously observed codes and protocols. We love our traditions, even our rigmarole, every bit as much as the next guy, only ours is earthy, rustic, folksy.

So I changed my mind about liturgy. It certainly can become dull and rote, but so can anything—water polo, rose gardening, kite flying, even lovemaking. Even fly-fishing. Just as often, though, maybe more so, liturgy can enrich these things. At its best, liturgy comprises the *gestures by which we honor* transcendent reality. It helps us give concrete expression to deepest convictions. It gives us choreography for things unseen and allows us to brush heaven among the shades of earth.

Our most significant relationships and events have a liturgical shape to them. They have rites of passage. Birthdays and homecomings, graduations and good-byes, Thanksgiving and Christmas and Easter, birth and death and marriage: all are marked by words and actions, songs and symbols, customs and traditions that enact them and complete them. And all these things also provide us with a means of entering them. What is a birthday without a cake, at least one candle burning on it, and a huddle of well-wishers, wearing clownish hats, singing in their ragged, hoary voices?

What is a birthday without liturgy?

What liturgy accomplishes is nothing short of astonishing: It breaks open the transcendent within the ordinary and the everyday. It lets us glimpse the deeper reality—the timeless things, the universal ones, the things above—within this particular instance of it.

Liturgy's an odd word, even awkward, for the early church to have chosen to describe its acts and forms of worship. It was a word they had to pry loose and drag over from a context far removed from the world of hymns and prayers and sermons. *Liturgy* originally meant a public work—something accomplished by a community for the community. A town bridge, for instance, or a village well, or a city wall: something built by the people and for the people. The oddness and awkwardness of the church's decision to import this word is even greater when we realize that they had a word for worship close at hand, a word in wide circulation within a religious context: *orgy*. Orgy now has sordid overtones. But in the days of the early church, it didn't, or at least the sordidness was still in the background. Orgy described a public event that produced a private, usually ecstatic, experience. It was the word pagan religions used for their worship, regardless of how many people were involved—and the more, the better—the emphasis was always squarely on the emotional experience of the individual.

It was all about *me*.

Not so liturgy. Liturgy is done *by me*—I am invited, perhaps required, to play a role—but it's not *about me*. It's about *us*. It is about *the Other*. Its purpose is to benefit the entire community—to provide protection or access to all. One of the more common uses of the word in the ancient world was for the making of a bridge. Liturgy is bridge building. It is to construct something that spans separate worlds and provides an efficient means of crossing from one to the other.

So it's a good word for what I want to describe here: the ways we might, individually and together, create access and protection for one another. The ways we might build and use a bridge for getting from where we are to where we want to be.

Liturgy is not law. This is important. The last thing I want to do here is return us to some parched and crabbed legalism around Sabbath observance. The beauty of calling Sabbath practice a liturgy is that nothing is violated if it's not followed, or if it's altered, expanded, abbreviated. No punishment ensues. Liturgy functions in a completely different way. Better to think of it, not just as a bridge, but as a kind of choreography, a choreography for our dance with things unseen, things ancient and things anticipated, things above and things below. Some move through this choreography with light-footed elegance, others with flat-footed clumsiness. You can add your own steps and moves, ignore others, or sit it out entirely. No one will arrest you.

But don't you want to dance?

Don't you want to push beyond mere idea and theory into the realm of the actual? I don't know how many books I've read or sermons I've heard (and too many I've preached) that have helped me think better but not live better. Though many abound in insight, they are bereft of practicality. They never go far enough, the writer or speaker, for fear, maybe, of being legalistic, shies away from actually suggesting ways to embody the idea, the theory.

This is where liturgy helps. Liturgy is a repertoire of *possible* ways—not the only way, or even the best way, but at least *some* way—to set what we know in motion. It lets us render thinking into doing, to pour our knowledge through our limbs. And it gives this with freedom both to imitate and to improvise. Though it describes a way of doing things, it never prescribes the way. Each person on each occasion is free to mimic what has come before, and free to innovate it. Each occurrence of liturgy is unique, unrepeatable, and yet is also enfolded with all the other occurrences. My dance will be both similar to and different from yours. It will echo yours, but with its own style, and rhythm, and pace.

So think of the Sabbath Liturgy sections in this book as choreographic notes. They are not to be followed slavishly. They are hints and prompts and invitations. They're meant to try to coax you onto the dance floor, to help you limber up, to get you to move in ways you might at first think awkward or foolhardy.

But who knows? After much practice, you might come to like it, even finding yourself, like Fred Astaire and Ginger Rogers, floating above the hard, cold floor of your workaday life, your feet barely touching.

ONE

WORK:
One Thing Before You Stop

You don't like your job.

It may be a good job. It may be engaging, rewarding, varied, with a fine balance of thrill and ease, intensity and serenity. It may be a job that calls for your creativity but doesn't overtax it, demands your vigilance but applauds it even more, requires your diligence but pays for it lavishly. It may give you a sense of power and virtue and importance and provide for you sleek cars and exotic rugs and handcrafted furniture and trips to warm places while everyone else is scraping thick rinds of ice from their windshields.

Still, you don't like it, at least not always. Some days you do, that's true. Some days you stretch out into it like a wild horse loosed after a tethering, thundering across open plain, gaining fresh strength with each stride.

But some days it's not like that at all. You're more like a wild horse haltered, corralled, backed into a stall. It's more like dressing in wet denim, like having a root canal without anaesthetic. You have more of these days than you like to admit—when the work is a fistful of thistles, and you dream of being someone else somewhere else doing something else.

I know.

I read it.

Not in something you wrote—I haven't snooped in your journal or intercepted your e-mail. I read it elsewhere, in something God wrote: Genesis. Genesis is about origins, about how most things began—earth and earthworms, family and family feuds, liturgy and metallurgy. And it's the story of the origins of work.

And of how we hate our work.

It begins well, the work. God speaks a resplendent creation into being, a world he exclaims over, again and again, "It is good!" And then he makes a man, who is "very good"! And then: "The LORD God took the man and put him in the Garden of Eden *to work it and take care of it*" (Gen. 2:15, emphasis mine).

The work is good, like everything else.

Then God sees one thing not good amidst all this goodness: the man's aloneness. So he makes a woman. Her God-given role is not first sexual or social. It's vocational: she's to be the man's helpmate. Her created purpose is to join the man in his work.

The work is good.

But matters go quickly awry. A serpent. A deception. A betrayal. A trespass. A concealment. A blaming. And in a twinkling, the party's over. God expels the man and woman from the garden. Many things are lost to them in this banishment: intimacy with each other and with God, nakedness without shame, the profuse abundance of Eden.

But not the work. There's still work to do, now more than ever. Only now this:

> Cursed is the ground because of you;
>   through painful toil you will eat of it
>   all the days of your life.
> It will produce thorns and thistles for you,
>   and you will eat the plants of the field.
> By the sweat of your brow

you will eat your food
until you return to the ground. (Genesis 3:17–19)

Sin makes the earth prickly. It entangles its beauty in brambles. Now, even the best the world has to offer—friendship, lovemaking, feather-down pillows, bluegrass music, Cajun shrimp—is affected in some way.

Including—especially—our work. *Through painful toil you will eat of it all the days of your life.*

Work doesn't work. It's broken. The Fall skewed what God created for good. Once—for one hour or one day or one month, who knows—there was a perfect fit between a man and a woman and the work they did. But ever after there's been a misfit. Now, doing our work is often like trying to build something with the wrong tool: sawing wood with a hammer, turning screws with a tape measure, pulling nails with a crescent wrench. Frustration is coded into the very structure of the fallen creation (see Rom. 8:18–21).

All this is to say: you can't help but not like your job some days. God made it that way.

There is no end of advice on how to endure work we don't like. The cartoon character Dilbert, lampooner of workplace politics, offers his counsel: "Eat one live toad the first thing in the morning, and nothing worse will happen to you the rest of the day."[1]

Or there's this:

> When you have had one of those take-this-job-and-shove-it-days, try this. On your way home, stop at your pharmacy and go to the section where they have thermometers. You will need to purchase a rectal thermometer made by the Q-tip Company. Be sure that you get this brand. When you get home, lock your doors, draw the drapes, and disconnect the phone so you will not be disturbed during your therapy. Change into something comfortable, such as a sweat suit, and

> lie down on your bed. Open the package containing the thermometer, remove it, and carefully place it on the bedside table so that it will not become chipped or broken. Take the written material that accompanies the thermometer. As you read, notice in small print this statement: "Every rectal thermometer made by Q-tip is *personally* tested."
>
> Close your eyes. Say out loud five times, "Thank you, oh thank you, that I do not work in quality control at the Q-tip Company."[2]

As funny as such advice is—and maybe, in a cockeyed way, as wise—there is a better way.

There's what God thinks about work.

Before we appreciate God's gift of rest, it is vital we appreciate his gift of work. We spend most of our lives working. And when we're not working, we spend most of that time thinking about it—complaining about it, fretting about it, preparing for it, recovering from it. We feel guilty when we don't do enough, resentful when we do too much.

One of the many books by oral historian Studs Terkel is entitled *Working*. It is a compilation of interviews with hundreds of people about their jobs. A common theme: "Most people . . . live somewhere between a grudging acceptance of their job and an active dislike of it."[3]

And yet most people, he found, are obsessed with their jobs. Work consumes them.

Most people deal with it, not by eating live toads daily or buying boxes of rectal thermometers, but by nursing a fantasy. It is the dream of being a man-child: escaping all obligation, all responsibility, but without losing a single shred of freedom. It is having ample money, time, health, power, and yet not one thing making a single claim on any of it.

My version of the dream is simple, modest even: a writing lodge near the ocean, within walking distance of a bakery that makes scones fresh every morning and serves strong, rich coffee, piping hot, with steamed milk and raw sugar. My lodge has a wood fireplace made from river rock, manteled with driftwood. It has a writing desk handcrafted from cherry or teak, set in front of a large window that looks out on rock and sky and water. In the morning, deer come and graze on grass tufts that bristle up among the stones. It has easy chairs, leather ones, and a matching couch where I can lie down a spell if needed. I spend my mornings writing, my afternoons walking, splitting wood, making bookshelves, reading poems. In the evening, my family materializes—magically—and we enjoy home-cooked food, games, ambling conversations. Sometimes we invite friends to join us. They always go home at a decent hour. We get plenty of sleep. I travel only to interesting places, when it's convenient for me, when I need a change of pace and scenery.

It's a lovely dream, an idyll, really.

But my suspicion is that it fits under the category of Isaiah's condemnation of Israel:

> In repentance and rest is your salvation,
> in quietness and trust is your strength,
> but you would have none of it.
> You said, "No, we will flee on horses."
> Therefore you will flee! (Isaiah 30:15–16)

A typical response to threat and burden is to want to flee it. It's evacuation as the cure for trouble. *If only I could get away* is our mantra. *Then I would be safe. Then I could enjoy my life.* But what we find is that flight becomes captivity: once we begin to flee the things that threaten and burden us, there is no end to fleeing.

God's solution is surprising. He offers rest. But it's a unique form of rest. It's to rest in him in the midst of our threats and our burdens. It's discovering, as David did in seasons of distress, that God is our rock and refuge right in the thick of our situation.

God, in other words, offers something better than our fantasy: he offers himself. "Come to Me, all who are weary and heavy-laden, and I will give you rest" (Matt. 11:28 NASB).

The argument of this book is that we uniquely take up his invitation by keeping Sabbath, both as a day and as an attitude. Those who remember the Sabbath and keep it holy don't need an idyll. They discover, in Rabbi Abraham Heschel's words, that they already "have heaven, and everything else besides."[4] They learn the art of sanctifying time—making, in Heschel's words again, a "sanctuary in time"—and so possess all the freedom and time they need.

But let me return to work. In order to keep the Sabbath well—to embrace the rest of God—we need a right view of work. Without a rich theology of labor, we'll have an impoverished theology of rest. We'll find that both are hectic, sporadic, chaotic. We'll find no joy in either.

I talked recently with a retired pastor who had served in various churches for forty-six years. For the past three he'd been retired.

"What are you up to these days?" I asked him.

"Not much," he said. "I'm still recovering."

"Oh. Did you have an accident, or surgery, or . . . ?"

"No. I mean recovering from ministry. I guess I never learned how to let things go. I carried the church's problems always, everywhere. I got so bottled up with it. Then I'd go on vacation and fall to pieces. It was like lapsing into a coma, or trying to break a drug addiction. I got sick. I wasn't able to sleep, or I couldn't wake up. I got angry and depressed. I withdrew. Coming back, I was almost paralyzed. I begged God to let me go, let me do anything else but this. Only I had no motivation for anything. I'm still getting over that."

Before we understand God's rest, we must understand the Lord's work.

The church has done little to help people here. Generally, we have a rickety theology of work. I can prove this in ten seconds. If I say the phrase "the Lord's work," what comes to mind?

If you're like most people, your default image here is of a pastor or priest or missionary doing pastoral, priestly, missionary things.

But this is a shallow and narrow understanding of the Lord's work. The Bible has a much deeper and richer perspective:

> One day as Jesus was standing by the Lake of Gennesaret, with the people crowding around him and listening to the word of God, he saw at the water's edge two boats, left there by the fishermen, who were washing their nets. He got into one of the boats, the one belonging to Simon, and asked him to put out a little from shore. Then he sat down and taught the people from the boat.
>
> When he had finished speaking, he said to Simon, "Put out into deep water, and let down the nets for a catch."
>
> Simon answered, "Master, we've been working hard all night and haven't caught anything. But because you say so, I will let down the nets."
>
> When they had done so, they caught such a large number of fish that their nets began to break. So they signaled their partners in the other boat to come and help them, and they came and filled both boats so full that they began to sink.
>
> When Simon Peter saw this, he fell at Jesus' knees and said, "Go away from me, Lord; I am a sinful man!" For he and all his companions were astonished at the catch of fish they had taken, and so were James and John, the sons of Zebedee, Simon's partners.
>
> Then Jesus said to Simon, "Don't be afraid; from now on you will catch men." So they pulled their boats up on shore, left everything and followed him. (Luke 5:1–11)

In some ways, this story reinforces our simplistic, one-dimensional view about "the Lord's work." It seems to indicate that workaday work—mending nets, patching boats, catching and lugging and gutting and selling fish—is beneath our dignity. It appears that Jesus demeans that kind of work—*no more fishing for fish*—and in contrast elevates the work of preaching and evangelizing. *From now on, fish for men.*

I want to turn that reading on its head.

The issue is not that Jesus values some types of work above others. That reading would destroy almost everything else the Bible says about work. The issue, plain and simple, is this: *what has Christ called you to do?* Has he called you to preach? Then leave the fish and the fishing boats, and go. Stop making excuses, seeking evasions. Dump it, and go.

But what if he's called you to fish? Or govern? Or fill teeth? Or collect garbage? Or grow cabbage? Someone has to do these things. This work can be a calling, a *vocation*—literally, the work that the Voice told you to do—every bit as much as a missionary's or a pastor's work can be (and, similarly, a missionary's or pastor's work is merely a job if the Voice isn't in it). When I have a toothache or a blown gasket or a hankering for fried chicken, I rejoice that not all are called to the work I do.

The passage from Luke 5 actually exalts honest work. Jesus goes onto the boat with these men. The boat serves as a makeshift pulpit from which Jesus preaches. But that's not good enough for Jesus, he wants to see this boat doing what it was designed to do. He wants to go fishing. A man after my own heart.

And next they're hauling up from water's depth a cornucopia of fish: so many, their tails and heads are like a thousand wriggling fingers half-thrust through net holes, their bodies sprawling wet and spangled across the boat's worn deck.

Here's the catch. (No pun intended. Okay—a bit of pun intended.) This is where we see that Jesus held honest work in highest regard—that far from brushing off the value of fishing in this instance, he was making a deliberate statement about its worth. (Besides which, Jesus had a hearty appetite for fish—he was always cooking or serving or gnawing on a piece of haddock or trout or whatever. Those fish had to have come from someone's nets, someone's hands. He could hardly have been out to shut down the fishing industry.)

Is it not strange that Jesus bothered to fill these men's nets in the first place? Their recent fishing expedition was a disaster, an exercise in humiliation and futility: up all night, casting and hauling, only muddy boots and rags of weed to show for it. And torn nets. That's how Jesus first finds these men, mending their nets. It's a bad day on the job when the equipment comes up both empty *and* broken. Before they can return home, draw a bath, take a meal, curl up in bed, they must do this finicky repair work.

They hate their job at this moment, I'm guessing. They want nothing more than a quick excuse to shuck the whole sorry enterprise, to tell the boss, "Take this job and shove it! I'd rather work at the Q-tip factory!" This is misery and drudgery. The pay is pathetic. The hours unholy. The benefits nonexistent. The conditions unsafe and unsanitary.

At it all night, and we haven't caught a thing. If Jesus wanted to make a statement about the relative worthlessness of mere fishing, he would have called them away from it while they still stood at the lakeshore, net mending. *Listen, men. The work you're presently doing—it's useless. Wasteful. God's blessing's not on it, isn't that obvious? Why bother? You want real work? I'll give you the kind of work that God cares about. The Lord's work. I'll make you preachers. Yes, the world needs more preachers.*

If Jesus had said that, we might reasonably conclude that he saw little value in fisherman's work.

But he doesn't say that. He says, "Let's go catch some fish."

"Aw!" Peter whines. "Do we have to? This job's the pits. I'm tired—tired of this work, tired of failing, just plain tired. But all right. If you say so."

They push off. They cast the nets—and suddenly, it's Christmas morning. Suddenly, this is the best job in the whole world. *I love my work.* Peter breaks into a rousing rendition of "Thank God It's Monday."

Then he stops. He looks at Jesus, Jesus looks at him, and Peter cowers. "Don't be afraid," Jesus says. "From now on you'll follow me."

Jesus, I'm convinced, wanted to elevate the status of these men's work in their own eyes so that he could reinforce a lesson about the cost of obedience. Jesus makes the choice to heed his voice costly. Fishing is suddenly good. It's suddenly hard to leave.

This is not a story about what kind of work Jesus values more, fishing for fish or fishing for men. Both are excellent, God-honoring ways to spend a day. He's saying, *I can make fishing for fish enjoyable and profitable. I can redeem it from the wearying and frustrating routine it's become for you. I can make it delightful. I'll do all that so you will gain a renewed appreciation for your work, and a deeper understanding of what I'm asking you to do. From the beginning, I will teach you the cost of discipleship.*

This is a story about calling. If Jesus calls you to be a fisher of fish, then do it with all your heart. Because he says so.

But if he calls you elsewhere, then do that without looking back. Don't be afraid. Because he says so.

The rest of Scripture supports this. God values our work and wants us to value it likewise. Adam was a gardener, a landscaper, a farmer, a taxonomer, a poet.

In all these things, he was doing the Lord's work.

Or consider Moses. His dying prayer ends with this plea to God: "Establish the work of our hands for us— / yes, establish the work of our hands" (Ps. 90:17). For Moses, the chief evidence of God's favor was what he did with the people's work. Did he take the labor of their hands—plowing, seeding, harvesting, building, raising children—and establish it, make it last, make it count?

Did he take their work and make it the Lord's work?

Most of his life Jesus was a carpenter. The apostle Paul, even at the height of his preaching and missionary activity, supported himself through tent making. Paul was so insistent about the value of common labor that he told the Thessalonians, "Make it your ambition . . . to work with your hands, just as we told you"; "We gave you this rule: 'If a man will not work, he shall not eat'" (1 Thess. 4:11; 2 Thess. 3:10). And yet Paul, along with this, also celebrated that the Thessalonians were evangelists and preachers, that the Lord's message "rang out" from them (1 Thess. 1:8). In his thinking, these vocations easily coexist.

It's all the Lord's work.

The Protestant reformer Martin Luther put it well:

> The maid who sweeps her kitchen is doing the will of God just as much as the monk who prays—not because she may sing a Christian hymn as she sweeps but because God loves clean floors. The Christian shoemaker does his Christian duty not by putting little crosses on the shoes, but by making good shoes, because God is interested in good craftsmanship.

Os Guinness, in his book *The Call*, tells the story of Jane Lucretia D'Esterre, a young mother and widow living in Scotland in the 1800s. Jane fell into despair over difficult circumstances and one dark day went down to the river to drown herself. But as she stood on the bridge, she looked up. She saw a field across the river, and in it a young man plowing. He worked with such skill and care and concentration that she became absorbed in the sight of it. Her fascination turned to wonder, and her wonder to thanksgiving, and her thanksgiving to a sense of purpose. She rose, went forth, and lived a long and productive life.[5]

She simply saw a man about the Lord's work.

There is sanctity in honest work. There is something in it that pleases, not just the eyes of man, but the heart of God:

> Each one should retain the place in life that the Lord assigned to him and to which God has called him. This is the rule I lay down in all the churches. . . . Each one should remain in the

PITKIN COUNTY LIBRARY
120 NORTH MILL
ASPEN CO 81611

> situation which he was in when God called him. Were you a slave when you were called? Don't let it trouble you—although if you can gain your freedom, do so. For he who was a slave when he was called by the Lord is the Lord's freedman; similarly, he who was a free man when he was called is Christ's slave. You were bought at a price; do not become slaves of men. Brothers, each man, as responsible to God, should remain in the situation God called him to. (1 Corinthians 7:17, 20–24)

A common problem in the early days of the church was that when a slave became a believer, he then assumed that the Lord wouldn't have him do something so menial and beneath his dignity as slave work.

But Paul thought otherwise:

> Slaves, obey your earthly masters with respect and fear, and with sincerity of heart, just as you would obey Christ. Obey them not only to win their favor when their eye is on you, but like slaves of Christ, doing the will of God from your heart. Serve wholeheartedly, as if you were serving the Lord, not men, because you know that the Lord will reward everyone for whatever good he does, whether he is slave or free. (Ephesians 6:5–8)

The opposite of a slave is not a free man. It's a worshiper. The one who is most free is the one who turns the work of his hands into sacrament, into offering. All he makes and all he does are gifts from God, through God, and to God. Just as simple bread and juice, when we eat and drink them in a spirit of thanksgiving and faith, become the very presence of Christ, so simple tasks—preparing sermons, cooking soup, cutting grass, growing corn—when done in the same spirit, are holy. It is all the Lord's work. Virtually any job, no matter how grueling or tedious—any job that is not criminal or sinful—can be a gift from God, through God, and to God. The work of our hands, by the alchemy of our devotion, becomes the worship of our hearts.

And more. Work done in such a spirit has the power to reveal Christ himself. It not only makes Christ attractive, *it makes Christ known.* Jesus showed the full extent of his love by washing his disciples' feet. He loved them by performing an act of servanthood so menial, so abased, that it was customarily assigned to the lowest household slave. At their final meal together, as his followers were still jockeying for pride of place, Jesus became their servant. Peter or Bartholomew or John or Judas—it was unthinkable that one of them would have lowered himself to this. *Better it be left undone than I stoop this low.* It was completely beyond all they asked or imagined that their Master and their Teacher—their Lord—would do it: that he would bow down and cradle in his hands, one by one, their cracked and dusty feet, blistered and calloused and reeking of roadways. That he'd ladle cool water on them, rubbing the dirt loose in his palms.

But that's what he did. That's how he showed the full extent of his love. And he told us we would be blessed if we did this also.

That's the Lord's work.

What kind of work do you do?

Sabbath Liturgy: Establishing the Work of Your Hands

My first real job, beyond household chores, was delivering daily newspapers to over a hundred mailboxes. Some of my route sprawled through a semirural area—tar-papered houses in fields of stone and scrub, with a droop-bellied horse or a spindly legged goat idling about, a yappy dog on the loose. I walked that route a thousand times. I walked it in blazes of sunshine and in blizzards of snow. I walked it beneath the heavens' benediction and the sky's cursing, over earth hard with cold or soft with mud. The thin strap of my carrier bag cut a nearly indelible groove into my shoulder. Some days in school I sat at my desk and rubbed my collarbone like an amulet, hoping to coax the soreness from it, to caress strength into it.

I learned early to hate work. Long before I ever read Genesis 3 and the hex God put on our labor—a thorny and sweaty thing it is—I understood full well anyhow. Those papers smudged my hands black with ink. They left my back cramped and aching. Many times I was attacked by dogs. On occasion I was cursed out by someone who found his paper wind-tossed or rain-drenched when he went to fetch it.

My father taught me to work hard, to bend my shoulder to a task until I finished it, regardless of how wearying or tedious it was. He instilled in me a solid work ethic and an attitude equivalent to what the apostle Paul taught the Thessalonians: *if you don't work, you won't eat.*

But he never said you had to like it, or if he did, I missed that lesson.

After I had been through several jobs—gas jockey, short-order cook, house painter, grocery boy, baker's helper—and found some reason, several reasons, to despise them all, I began to wonder if there was a better way.

There was. The apostle Paul, instructing slaves, became my teacher. His best and most enduring lesson was this: whatever you can do with a clean conscience, you can do to the glory of God. No work is so menial that it cannot be rendered as worship. As I began to knead the reality of that truth into the details of my tasks, my attitude changed dramatically. I found joy in toil. My attitude, once toxic, turned tonic. I was not just inspired for the work; I became, for others, inspiring in it.

What if your work became worship? What if the work of your hands—repairing lawn mowers, scouring pots, paving streets, mending bones, balancing ledgers—was Eucharistic, a sacrament of God's presence that you gave and received? What if Jesus himself was your boss, the One who watched over you and whom you honored with your efforts?

Here's a radical idea: next time you're tempted to complain about your work, praise God for it instead. Next time you open your mouth to gossip about people you work with or smear those you work for, stop yourself and turn in the other direction: pray for them, thank God for them, find the good in them. Next time you want to quit, pour that into worship.

Why not right now? Put down the book and take up, Eucharist-like, the work of your hands. Lift it to God. Receive it with thanksgiving. Offer it with sincerity. Name the ways this work has blessed you, provided for you, allowed you to be a blessing. Pray for those you work with—your employees, your employers, your colleagues, your clients. Look at the things around you that your work has provided: the clothes you wear, the shoes you walk in, the food in fridge and cupboard, the table you eat at, the car you drive. Even if it's not much, it's more than nothing. Say something like this: "God, I praise you that there is food to spare in this home. I praise you that I was able to pay the electric bill this month to cook that food and had a chair I could sit in to partake of it."

God wants to establish the work of your hands, but he's asking you to lend a hand.

TWO

A Beautiful Mind: *Stopping to Think Anew*

In my early days as a pastor, I possessed a dangerous combination of naiveté and cockiness. I was untrained for this work—it's a long story—and yet somehow that produced in me the opposite effect of what it should have. Instead of modesty, I exuded brashness, and instead of caution, rashness. I was a mix of foolhardy and swagger. I had my Bible, a couple of arts degrees, a gift for gab.

What more did I need?

So when a woman called about her twelve-year-old stepson, Jason, and described to me his unruliness, I confidently assured her that a quick session or two with me would fix the problem.

The next day, the woman and Jason showed up in my office. They typically had nothing to do with churches or pastors, but the woman was desperate and broke and had nowhere else to turn. She sat at seat's edge, weary and jittery, words scattering from her like flak. Jason slumped in his chair, sullen and monosyllabic.

The stepmom recited a litany of the stepson's wrongdoing: Outright defiance. Abusive language. Extreme withdrawal. Vandalism—smashing plates, kicking holes in walls and doors, keying cars, thrashing the cat. Threats and violence toward her and her daughter. Stealing money from her purse. Stealing her jewelry and pawning it. Cannabis seeds in his jeans pockets. And now, what had prompted the call, getting caught shoplifting. The police had brought him home handcuffed.

After five minutes of this, I knew I was out of my depth.

The stepmom kept cataloging, with mounting shrillness, Jason's myriad and random acts of badness (all the while he sat there limp and silent, as though dying from a bullet wound). Then she stopped. She was ready now for me to fix it all, just as I'd promised.

I swallowed hard and said, "Um."

I shuffled the papers on my desk. I arranged the pens there in interesting geometrical designs: squares, triangles, hexagons, intersected diamonds. I took a breath and said, "Um."

And then, slowly and piecemeal, just playing for time, I began to sort out the story of how they ended up in the same household. It was a tale of family brokenness stretching back for generations. Jason's mother was a drug addict, and later a prostitute. She had Jason when she was only a teenager and left him and his father when Jason was only months old.

Later, when Jason was about five years old, she came back. By then Jason's father had remarried, and the stepmom—this woman before me—was caring for the boy. But Jason's birth mother wanted her baby back. She wanted to be a good mom. She wanted to start a home, settle down, make a life for both of them.

And she tried. She tried for almost a month. But she was overwhelmed by it. She got angry at every little thing. She resented the money and time it took to be a parent. She was dangerously negligent, leaving Jason alone while she went out with her male friends.

Three weeks into it, she abandoned the idea of motherhood. She left once more, never to be seen or heard from since.

Now I was really out of my depth. My temptation was to look at my watch, announce their hour was up, thank them for coming, and show them the door. Instead, I started praying, eyes open: "Oh God, what now? It's my turn. I'm supposed to be wise. I'm supposed to help these people. But I've got nothing to give. Lord, you see their plight. You see mine. I'm sorry I thought I was equal to this. I'm not. You are. Help."

And then I prayed this: "Lord, please give me the wisdom of Solomon."

What dropped into my head right then, bright as a coin falling into water, was a story about Solomon. Solomon, the Bible says, was the wisest man on earth. His wisdom surpassed all who came before him and all who came after. It was of such renown that kings and queens traveled from great distances to sit at Solomon's feet and drink in his words. It was of such enduring substance that, distilled into proverbs, it still guides parents, pastors, teachers, politicians, leaders.

Legendary wisdom.

But the Bible gives only one example of it in action. It's the story of two prostitutes who come to Solomon for a ruling. The girls have been roommates, each the mother of a son. One child has died. Both claim to be the mother of the surviving child. They've fought bitterly over this. Their grievance has reached the place where only the wisest man in the world can bring resolution.

And so they seek audience with Solomon. The women's rivalry and controversy are so combustible they erupt right there, in the king's court. In response, the king himself erupts. "Bring me a sword!" he hollers. "Cut this child in two; give half to each."

This from the wisest man on earth.

I'm praying with my eyes open, asking for the wisdom of Solomon, and in pops this story. I'm puzzled. It seems to me that Solomon just wanted this thing over with, these squabbling women and this squalling child out of his way—not unlike my wanting Jason and his stepmom gone. It seems to me he's merely run out of patience.

Then the lights go on.

"Jason," I say, "look at me."

He does, halfhearted.

"No, Jason. Really look at me. I need you to listen very carefully."

A slight stirring beneath the crust of his apathy.

"Are you listening?"

He nods.

"All right. There's a story in the Bible about a king, a very wise king, so wise that everyone in the whole earth sought his wisdom. His name was Solomon. Ever heard about him?"

No.

"Well," I continue, "he was very wise. But there's only one story we have to prove it. It's a strange story, about two women with one child. Both claim to be the child's mother. Neither will give way—and, of course, they both can't be the mother, can they?"

No.

"Right. So the two women come to this wise king Solomon to have him sort it out. Now, if I were Solomon, here's what I'd do: I'd order an investigation. I'd call for DNA tests. Or I'd cross-examine these two women with such skill and cunning that I'd tease out one or the other's deceit.

"But Solomon doesn't do this. He does something that seems reckless. He asks for a sword and proposes to cut the baby in two and give half to each woman."

I pause. The story's oddness blooms thick in the silence.

"Jason, are you still listening?"

Yes.

"A funny thing happens next. One of the women steps up and says, 'Oh, I'm sorry. I shouldn't have let this thing go this far. Give the baby to her.' See, Solomon calls their bluff, and it works.

"Now, Jason, I have a question. Ready?"

Yes.

"Who do you think was the real mother?"

Jason answered without blinking: "The woman who gave the child away."

"Jason, you're right. How did you know?"

"Well," he said, "because she didn't want the baby killed."

"Because she loved him?"

"Right," he said.

"Right," I said. "She loved her child so much, she'd rather see him alive and whole in another woman's arms than dead and dismembered in her own.

"Jason, was that your mother? Was that what she did with you? She'd rather lose you by giving you away than lose you in a worse way by trying to keep you?"

The things you wish you had a camera for: Jason then. The way he sat straight up. The way light flooded him and his eyes brimmed with wonder and laughter. The way joy returned after years of exile, sudden and quiet and fleet. The way his face, scowling ugly a moment before, a bitter old man's face, turned youthful and hopeful. Jason was like a soldier standing in the soft glow of daybreak after a night of death raining down from the sky, astonished and thankful to be alive.

Yet I never changed one thing about Jason's circumstances. I never altered a single detail of his life.

The only thing I changed was his mind.

That day, it was enough to change everything.

Often we get this backward. We won't change our minds, won't revise our attitudes, until someone—God, a parent, a boss, a spouse, a child, a coworker—changes our circumstances. We refuse to budge until someone moves a mountain. Our lives shuttle between an alteration of *if only*, *what if*, and *as soon as*: *If only I had more money. As soon as I get a different job. What if my husband loved me more? If only my child wasn't rebellious. . . . As soon as . . . What if . . .*

But this is not how God works.

This is: "Be transformed *by the renewing of your mind*"; "Be made new *in the attitude of your minds*" (Rom. 12:2; Eph. 4:23, emphasis mine).

Under God's economy, *nothing really changes until our minds do.*

Transformation is the fruit of a changed outlook. First our minds are renewed, and then we are transformed, and then everything is different, even if it stays the same.

God is more interested in changing your thinking than in changing your circumstances. He wants you to have the same attitude as and the very mind of Jesus Christ (see Phil. 2:5–8). To pull that off is a miracle larger than splitting oceans or tossing mountains into them. It is akin to raising the dead. Yet this is the daily occupation of the Spirit—leading us into all truth, reminding us of the things Christ taught, taking the things of Christ and making them known to us again. And this is the one area above all where we are urged to keep in step with the Spirit—to move in the direction he's moving so that, seeing differently, we are free to live differently (see Gal. 5:22–25).

All this touches on the art of Sabbath-keeping. What makes Sabbath time—whether a day or a year, an afternoon or a week, a month or a moment—different from all other time? Simple: a shift in our thinking, an altering of our attitudes.

First we change our minds. Before we keep a Sabbath day, we cultivate a Sabbath heart.

A Sabbath heart sanctifies time. This is not a ritual. It's a perspective. And it's not a shift in circumstances—you still have the same job tomorrow, the same problems with your aging parents or wayward children, the same battle looming in the church. But you make a deliberate choice to shift point of view, to come at your circumstances from a fresh angle and with greater depth of field. You choose to see your life otherwise, through a different lens, from a different standpoint, with a different mind-set.

The root of the Hebrew word for "sanctify" means "to betroth." It is to pledge marriage. It is to choose to commit yourself, all of yourself, to *this* man or *this* woman, and then to honor that commitment in season and out. Sanctifying time works the same way. You pledge to commit yourself, all of yourself, to *this* time, and then you honor that commitment whether it's convenient or not.

The story of the first man and woman helps us understand this. When God sees and laments Adam's aloneness and decides to make a woman for him, he doesn't move directly from decision to action. He hesitates. He orchestrates an interruption. He assigns Adam a task—a huge, intricate, unwieldy task, a task that, although it's narrated in a single line, may have taken days, weeks, or months to fulfill. God has Adam name all earth's creatures: giraffes, squids, wombats, marmots, centipedes, woodpeckers, steelheads, the three-toed sloth, the Sasquatch. Just as God spoke all creation into being, now he has Adam speak identity into all creation. He has him give voice to the whole pageant of earth.

Before intimacy, taxonomy.

It seems an odd, even cruel, thing for God to make Adam do. It would be one thing if there were no helpmate on the way, and all God wanted was to provide him a creative diversion, to distract him from his haunting aloneness. But God already knows what he's going to do. He's going to bring the man a beautiful woman, utterly naked, bone of his bone and flesh of his flesh. Why not cut to the chase and do it now?

The naming, I think, is a testing.

And like all good tests, it's designed to sharpen something in the man, to seal a resolve: that there is no other creature in all creation with whom he can forge a companionship rich enough to banish his aloneness. What about that golden retriever? He's always glad to see you, no matter how late you come home or how boorish and neglectful you've been. He seems oblivious to your glaring inadequacies. Or what about the horse? He's loyal and trusting, and he surrenders his power to your will, though your strength is paltry next to his. Or what about that cat?

Well, maybe that's stretching things.

But it's not the dog, and not the horse, and certainly not the cat who can solve the man's plight.

Only the woman will do.

He must see her as the only one in all creation who can end the tyranny of his aloneness. Only she is close as his rib bone, close as his own breathing. For her alone should he leave mother and father.[1] With her alone can he be naked without shame.

That is the art of sanctifying. That is what it means to betroth another.

Just so with Sabbath time. Sabbath is time sanctified, time betrothed, time we perceive and receive and approach differently from all other time. Sabbath time is unlike every and any other time on the clock and the calendar. We are more intimate with it. We are more thankful for it. We are more protective of it and generous with it. We become more ourselves in the presence of Sabbath: more vulnerable, less afraid. More ready to confess, to be silent, to be small, to be valiant.

There is no day in all creation that can banish our aloneness, even while meeting us in it, like this day.

But first we change our minds.

One of the largest obstacles to true Sabbath-keeping is leisure. It is what cultural historian Witold Rybczynski calls "waiting for the weekend," where we see work as only an extended interlude between our real lives. Leisure is what Sabbath becomes when we no longer know how to sanctify time. Leisure is Sabbath bereft of the sacred. It is a vacation—literally, a vacating, an evacuation. As Rybczynski sees it, leisure has become despotic in our age, enslaving us and exhausting us, demanding from us more than it gives.[2]

We all know how unsatisfying mere leisure can be. We've all known what it's like to return to the classroom or the workplace after a time spent in revelry or retreat, in high jinks or hibernation: typically, we go back weary and depressed, like jailbirds caught. The time away from work wasn't time sanctified so much as time stolen, time when we escaped for a short-lived escapade.

The difference between this and Sabbath couldn't be sharper.

Sanctifying some time adds richness to all time, just as an hour with the one you love brings light and levity to the hours that follow. To spend time with the object of your desire is to emerge, not sullen and peevish, but elated and refreshed. You come away filled, not depleted.

The Greeks understood. Embedded in their language, expressed in two distinct words for "time," is an intuition about the possibility of sanctified time. Time, they knew, has two faces, two natures. It exists in two separate realms, really, as two disparate dimensions, and we orient ourselves primarily to one or the other. One is sacred time, the other profane.

The first word is *chronos*—familiar to us because it's the root of many of our own words: *chronology*, *chronicle*, *chronic*. It is the time of clock and calendar, time as a gauntlet, time as a forced march. The word derives from one of the gods in the Greek pantheon. Chronos was a nasty minor deity, a glutton and a cannibal who gorged himself on his own children. He was always consuming, never consummated. Goya depicted him in his work *Chronos Devouring His Children*. In the painting, Chronos is gaunt and ravenous, wild-eyed with hunger. He crams a naked, bloody-stumped figure into his gaping mouth. Peter Paul Rubens depicted Chronos even more alarmingly: a father viciously biting into his son's chest and tearing the flesh away, the boy arching backward in shock and pain.

Chronos is the presiding deity of the driven.

The second Greek word is *kairos*. This is time as gift, as opportunity, as season. It is time pregnant with purpose. In *kairos* time you ask, not "What time is it?" but "What is this time *for*?" *Kairos* is the servant of holy purpose. "There is a time *for* everything," Ecclesiastes says, "and a season for every activity under heaven."

> A time to be born and a time to die,
> a time to plant and a time to uproot, . . .
> a time to embrace and a time to refrain,
> a time to search and a time to give up,

> a time to keep and a time to throw away, . . .
> a time to be silent and a time to speak,
> a time to love and a time to hate,
> a time for war and a time for peace. (3:1–2, 5–8)

This year, this day, this hour, this moment—each is ripe for something: Play. Work. Sleep. Love. Worship. Listening. Each moment enfolds transcendence, lays hold of a significance beyond itself. Ecclesiastes sums it up this way: "I have seen the burden God has laid on men. He has made everything beautiful in its time. He has also set eternity in the hearts of men; yet they cannot fathom what God has done from beginning to end" (3:10–11).

Chronos betrays us, always. It devours the beauty it creates. But sometimes *chronos* betrays itself: it stirs in us a longing for Something Else—Something that the beauty of things in time evokes but cannot satisfy. Either we end up as the man in Ecclesiastes did: driven, driven, driven, racing hard against *chronos*, desperate to seize beauty but always grasping smoke, ashes, thorns. Seeking purpose and finding none, only emptiness.

Or we learn to follow the scent of eternity in our hearts. We begin to orient toward *kairos*. We start to sanctify some of our time. And an odd thing can happen then. Purpose, even unsought, can take shape out of the smallest, simplest things: "I know that there is nothing better for men than to be happy and do good while they live. That everyone may eat and drink, and find satisfaction in all his toil—this is the gift of God" (Eccl. 3:12–13).

This is a gift of God: to experience the sacred amidst the commonplace—to taste heaven in our daily bread, a new heaven and new earth in a mouthful of wine, joy in the ache of our muscles or the sweat of our brows.

There's an exercise that some pilots go through late in their flight training. The student pilot gets the plane airborne, at cruising altitude.

Then the instructor places a loose-fitting, thick-woven sack over the student's head, so the student can see nothing. The instructor takes the controls and starts stunt-piloting: He loops the loop. He pushes the plane, Turkish-headache-style, skyward, then flips belly-up and swoops earthward. He rollicks and spirals, careens and nosedives, tailspins and wing-tilts. He gets the student utterly discombobulated. Then he puts the plane in a suicide dive, plucks the bag off the student's head, and hands him the controls. His job: to get the plane back under control.

The exercise is called Recovering from an Unusual Attitude.[3]

To keep Sabbath, most of us first have to recover from an unusual attitude. We find ourselves disoriented, in vertigo. We're dizzy with all our busyness and on a collision course.

Maybe it's time to change your mind: to stop feeding Chronos his own children and start sanctifying time.

Sabbath Liturgy: Taking Thoughts Captive

I sometimes imagine Solomon submitting the Proverbs to a modern publisher and getting this response:

> Dear Sol:
>
> Thanks for the opportunity to glance over your recent submission. We loved your dad's book and continue to be humbled and amazed by how many people it's blessed.
>
> About your book: there's some great stuff here—some real gems of insight (my four-year-old loved the one about a dog's vomit, though I'm not sure something like that would make the final cut). I also appreciate your ability to cover a wide range of topics with brevity. You explore everything from domestic squabbles to international politics to corporate strategy, and so succinctly (though, I admit, here and there a tad cryptically).
>
> But I need to be frank with you, Sol: this is an editorial nightmare. It is all over the place. One minute you're talking about nattering wives, the next about kings' hearts, and then suddenly you're on about table manners, lazy people, poor men, whatever. You repeat yourself in many places, contradict yourself in others. I'm intrigued but confused. I wish you would take one theme per chapter and develop it fully.
>
> I'm not saying no. But I am asking this: sum up the whole book in one clear sentence—I'm talking thesis statement here, Sol, just as in your college days. If we can nail that, I think we can build the book from there.
>
> Say hi to the wives and concubines and kids. And congratulations on your recent marriages last month.

Kindest regards,
Friendly Publisher

P.S. I should have mentioned, the title *The Proverbs* strikes me as a bit pedestrian. I'm thinking something catchier, like *Zingers: One-Liners to Delight Your Friends and Humiliate Your Enemies.* What do you think?

Solomon's response might have gone something like this:

Dear Friendly Publisher:

I've thought about your critique and request, and though I think you've missed the point of my book's (dis)organization (hint: it mimics life), I at least want to give you the "one clear" sentence that sums up the entire work. I simply lifted this straight out of my book. Here it is:

> The wisdom of the prudent is to give thought to their ways, but the folly of fools is deception. [Proverbs 14:8]

Hope that helps.

Shalom,
Solomon

P.S. I prefer the original title.

The wisdom of the wise is to give thought to their ways. *They think about where they're going.* But the folly of fools is deception. *They keep lying to themselves.*

Wise people ask, *Does the path I'm walking lead to a place I want to go? If I keep heading this way, will I like where I arrive?*

Fools don't ask that. They keep making excuses for themselves, justifying and blaming, all the way to nowhere. They dupe themselves right to the grave. They never change their minds.

Consider your ways. That's a wise Sabbath Liturgy. And let me make it even more specific: consider your thoughts and attitudes, the pattern of them, their shape and drift. Are they leading you where you want to go? Plot their trajectory: will they land you in a place you care to live?

If not, change your mind. "Take captive every thought to make it obedient to Christ" (2 Cor. 10:5).

Take a moment right now. Begin with David's prayer, "Search me, O God, and see if there be any wicked way in me" (see Ps. 139:23–24). Invite the Spirit to search you and reveal one habitual thought, one attitude of your heart, that is *mis*leading you. It may be shame, a sense that you must keep hiding, keep avoiding the light. It may be pride, or a temptation to judge others, or an insecurity that drives you into envy and rivalry. It may be just the sense of insignificance—that no one sees you, not even God.

It may be how you see God.

Whatever it is, ask God to change your mind. End with the rest of David's prayer: "And lead me in the way everlasting" (Ps. 139:24).

THREE

The Rest of God: *Stopping to Find What's Missing*

British Columbia is a land of forests and deserts and mountains and rivers. It is hemmed in on one side by the Pacific Ocean, most of the other side by the granite and glaciers of the Rocky Mountains, and held together by a patchwork of lakes, some tiny and icy and blue-green, others huge and dark and warm as a kiss. British Columbia was the wilderness that old gold prospectors, Yukon-bound, plied their way across in search of Aladdin's cave, surviving by hardiness and foolhardiness. These were men wily and stubborn, living by the skin of their teeth. But some didn't have to go to the Yukon. Some struck gold right here, in this province, in pockets where swift rivers spilled out of mountains, clawing loose rock and mineral on their way down, strewing their plunder through valleys where the water slowed and bent.

My wife's grandmother Alice used to live in a place like that, in a little town called Enderby. And in her middle years, in the late part of the twentieth century, men with lingering gold fever still went there to try to dredge up what they could from river silt. They still bored deep into the hills, propping up the earth with a rickety skeleton of rough-hewn timbers that almost always, at some twist in the tunnel, gave way.

One day Grandma was in her backyard, polishing a large stone. It was a boulder that sat athwart her garden, too big to move. It was one of those stones round and smooth, tumbled by eons of wind and ice and water, thickly embedded with glittery chunks of mineral. She was polishing it with sandpaper. Her logic was that, since she couldn't be rid of the thing, she may as well beautify it, try to remove the scumble of dullness on its surface and hone it to a lustrous sheen. She was going to make it the centerpiece of her garden.

But she got more than that. As she sanded, she noticed a thin sifting of gold gathering on the stone. She pressed the moist tip of her finger into it and pulled up a caking of gold dust. Her heart raced. She sanded faster, leaning her whole body into it, and more gold appeared. Now she was scrubbing that rock as if it were a bloodstain, with strong, sweeping strokes, bone and sinew bent to the work. Gold accumulated rapidly.

She caught the virus in one swoop. She understood with perfect instinct what all this time she'd dismissed as sheer nonsense: grown men squandering all else—homes and farms and families and reputations—and flinging themselves headlong into reckless escapades, spending their years burrowing beneath tree roots, grubbing through silt beds.

But now she had it too: gold fever. She was going to be rich.

She stopped a moment, to wipe her brow, to rest a spell. And that's when she noticed that something was wrong with her wedding ring. The topside was normal, but the underside, the part that nestled in the crease where her finger joined her palm, wasn't. The band there was thin as a cheese slicer wire, thin as a filament.

She had nearly sanded her wedding ring clean off. All that gold was merely filings. It was the remnants of her heirloom. It was her treasure reduced to dust.

It was all fool's gold.

I laughed the first time my wife told me that story, but only the first time. After that it made me sad. It's sad for its own sake, an aging woman giddy as a schoolgirl, heady with a sense of windfall, dreaming of a new dress and a real holiday, and the next moment crestfallen, stinging with shame over her coveting and naiveté.

But it's also sad because much of my own life I've repeated, again and again, Grandma Alice's mistake. I've squandered treasures in pursuit of dust. I've eroded precious, irreplaceable things in my efforts to extract something that's not actually there. I've imagined I'm on the trail of a groundbreaking discovery, only to find I'm at the tail end of a hard loss. Here are a few: all the times I never swam in a cool lake with my children, made a snowman or baked sugar cookies with them, lingered in bed with my wife on a Saturday morning, or helped a friend in need, all because I was in a hurry to—well, that's just it: I don't remember what.

I was just in a hurry.

I've been in a hurry most of my life. Always rushing to get from where I am to where I'm going. Always cocking my arm to check my watch, doing that habitually, mechanically, mindlessly. Always leaning heavy on the gas, in the passing lane, angry that the driver in front of me doesn't share my sense of urgency, that she's in no particular hurry and can't seem to imagine a world where anybody would be. Always fuming over having to wait in bank lines and grocery checkouts and road construction zones.

Sanding away my wedding band.

But all that hurry has gotten me no farther ahead. It's actually set me back. It's diminished me. My efforts to gain time have only lost it. Whole epochs of my existence have swept by me in a blur, with nary a cheap souvenir to remember them by. There are seasons and seasons of my life swallowed whole, buried in a black hole of forgetting.

I keep waking up, finding myself older, my children altered dramatically, the paint I just put on the side of the house a season or two ago already blistered and flaking. I can't remember getting here. My wife turned to me one evening not long ago and spoke a name. At first I was uncomprehending. The name was like a lost word, archaic, a word I used to bandy freely but now whose meaning I could not dredge up or pry open. Then I remembered: the name belonged to a man I once knew well—or thought I did. I had lost touch with him several years past. Until Cheryl mentioned him, I had forgotten him entirely. Now, I recalled him only in hazy silhouette, in rough fragments. His name was a smudge of memory. I could not remember the texture of his voice or the shape of his face, any of the conversations we'd had. I couldn't remember his middle name, or if he had one. I couldn't remember what secrets I entrusted to him, or he to me. I couldn't remember where he was born, who his parents were, where he now lived. These were all things I am quite sure I used to know.

I just must not have been fully present at the time I learned them. I was probably in a hurry, already pressing hard and anxious toward elsewhere, lacking patience to seal up what I'd gathered. A large chunk of my life disappeared, without a trace.

Someone asked me recently what was my biggest regret in life. I thought a moment, surveying the vast and cluttered landscape of my blunders and losses, the evil I have done and the evil that's been done against me.

"Being in a hurry," I said.

"Pardon?"

"Being in a hurry. Getting to the next thing without fully entering the thing in front of me. I cannot think of a single advantage I've ever gained from being in a hurry. But a thousand broken and missed things, tens of thousands, lie in the wake of all that rushing."

Through all that haste, I thought I was making up time. It turns out I was throwing it away.

Sanding away my wedding ring.

The Chinese join two characters to form a single pictograph for busyness: heart and killing.[1] That is stunningly incisive. The heart is the place the busy life exacts its steepest toll.

This is true literally, physically, cardiologically. My own father died of coronary failure, as did his brother before him. Both, in their own way, were busy, driven men. I didn't know my uncle well. He was the editor of a newspaper, a small-town daily. I imagine him living on coffee and cigarettes and greasy burgers, eaten from their waxy or foil wrappers, devoured standing up, between phone calls. I picture him chronically exhausted, habitually irritated, yelling and sighing too much, feeling the pressure of the next edition building before the current edition's even off the press. I think of him standing at his office window on a late winter's day, his reflection in the darkening window like a ghost looking back at him, pale and gray and thin, haunting him with what he's missed and with what he's become. I envision him afraid to slow down, lest he stop and the utter vanity of it all overwhelm him. He died young, in his early fifties. All that worry and cholesterol and caffeine and nicotine had become a muddy thickness in his blood.

My father worked in the oil industry, in corporate sales. It was a cutthroat business, multimillion-dollar accounts that danced on the pinhead of half-cent-per-liter discounts. His work consumed him. He could describe the viscosity of oil, the way it turned treacly in cold or watery in heat, with a rhetorical power that was dazzling. But it was his hateful obsession, he loathed it most days but couldn't let it go, couldn't stop brooding about it, competing with his rivals, striving after some nose-ahead victory. He was like this even when he was only driving a golf ball or driving the car to the lake. It was all a race or a contest to him. He sanded away his wedding ring.

The company he worked for retired him early, unfairly he thought, and so he spent many years afterward fighting an unwinnable court battle. When he finally slowed down, he seemed to collapse. He died at sixty-seven of a heart attack that felled him in a single blow. I was just getting to know him. Some nights I wake and wish, with an ache that's hard on my own heart, for just one more conversation between us. Some nights I dream of him. He is usually young, younger than I am, and relaxed in a way I rarely saw him. He is standing in an open space, where wind sweeps earth and air clean. He is smiling, not a wide, toothy smile, just a crimp at the corner of his mouth, a suture in his cheek. It is a smile of hidden mirth, a secret he holds that makes his heart light.

But his heart wasn't light. His heart killed him.

I miss him.

But this insight—that the busy life murders our hearts—is also true in other ways. Wayne Muller writes:

> I have visited the large offices of wealthy donors, the crowded rooms of social service agencies, and the small houses of the poorest families. Remarkably, within this mosaic there is a universal refrain: *I am so busy.* It does not seem to matter if the people I speak with are doctors or day-care workers, shopkeepers or social workers, parents or teachers, nurses or lawyers, students or therapists, community activists or cooks.
>
> Whether they are Hispanic or Native American, Caucasian or Black, the more their lives speed up, the more they feel hurt, frightened, and isolated. Despite their good hearts and equally good intentions, their work in the world rarely feels light, pleasant, or healing. Instead, as it all piles endlessly upon itself, the whole experience of being alive begins to melt into one enormous obligation. It becomes the standard greeting everywhere: *I am so busy.*[2]

And something dies in us. Too much work, the British used to say, makes Jack a dull boy. But it's worse than that. It numbs Jack, parches Jack, hardens Jack. It kills his heart. When we get too busy, everything becomes either a trudge or a scramble, the doldrums or sheer mayhem. We get bored with the familiar, threatened by the unfamiliar. Our capacity for both steadfastness and adventure shrivels.

We just want to be left alone.

One measure for whether or not you're rested enough—besides falling asleep in board meetings—is to ask yourself this: *How much do I care about the things I care about?* When we lose concern for people, both the lost and the found, for the bride of Christ, for friendship, for truth and beauty and goodness; when we cease to laugh when our children laugh (and instead yell at them to quiet down) or weep when our spouses weep (and instead wish they didn't get so emotional); when we hear news of trouble among our neighbors and our first thought is that we hope it isn't going to involve us—*when we stop caring about the things we care about*—that's a signal we're too busy. We have let ourselves be consumed by the things that feed the ego but starve the soul.

Busyness kills the heart.

And then the moment of reckoning comes—when we must meet the situation with genuine, heartfelt compassion, wisdom, courage—and nothing's there, only grim resignation and a dull resentment that we got dragged into this.

Wayne Muller writes on the fallout of the busy life:

> I have sat on dozens of boards and commissions with many fine, compassionate, and generous people who are so tired, overwhelmed, and overworked that they have neither the time nor the capacity to listen to the deeper voices that speak to the essence of the problems before them. Presented with the intricate and delicate problems of poverty, public health, community well-being, and crime, our impulse, born of weariness, is to rush headlong toward doing anything that will make the problem go away. Maybe then we can finally go home and get some rest.[3]

Busyness makes us stop caring about the things we care about.

And not only that. Busyness also robs us of knowing God the way we might.

It's true that some facets of God we glimpse only through motion. Only those who stretch out their hands and offer water to the thirsty discover, disguised among them, Jesus. Only those who trudge up the mountain, willing to grow blistered and weary on the narrow trail, witness his transfiguration. Only those who invite the stranger in to share bread realize they've entertained an angel unawares, sometimes even Christ himself. Often, God meets us along the way, as we go: he waits to see who will step out before he sidles up, woos us over, intercepts, redirects.

But other facets of God we discover only through stillness. "Be still," the psalm instructs, "and know that I am God" (Ps. 46:10). Only Mary, Martha's sister, sitting wide-eyed and open-eared, truly hosts Christ in her home. Only those who wait on the Lord renew their strength. Only those who are quiet and watchful find God's mercy that is new every morning. Only those who join him in his love for the contrite and broken in spirit recognize him hidden among "the least of these" (Matt. 25:40).

"He *makes me* lie down in green pastures," Psalm 23 says (v. 2, emphasis mine). If we don't choose to lie down, God sometimes *makes* us. That's happened to me more than once: I refused the sleep or rest he granted, and my health broke.

He made me lie down.

But only then was I still enough to hear God, to "taste and see" that he was good (Ps. 34:8).

A man in my church became sick and couldn't shake it. It went on for months. He was usually a man who went full tilt at everything, night and day. In Dr. Seuss's *The Cat in the Hat,* there's a page where that frolicsome, troublesome cat is pirouetting on a rubber ball while balancing a teetering mountain of stacked objects: a fishbowl on a rake, a tray with a milk jug on his free foot, a cake and a teacup on his hat, a toy boat on one hand and a tower of books on the other. He holds a Japanese fan in the curled tip of his tail. The cat claims he's capable of even greater feats than this. But:

> That is what the cat said . . .
> Then he fell on his head!
> He came down with a bump
> From up there on the ball.
> And Sally and I,
> We saw ALL the things fall.[4]

That's a suitable metaphor for this man's life.

The sickness stripped him down. The sickness collapsed him and scattered his circus act. He had to spend whole days and weeks housebound, idle, waiting, banking energy just to go up and down stairs. He spent more time with his wife and children in those few months than he had in all the years he'd known them. He read more than he ever had and pondered more and prayed more.

One day he said to me, "I know God is trying to get my attention. I just haven't figured out yet what he wants my attention for. He must want me to do something."

I thought a moment. "Maybe," I said, "that's the problem: you think he wants your attention *in order for you to do something.* Maybe he just wants your attention."

Maybe that's what God requires most from us: our attention.

Indeed, this is the essence of a Sabbath heart: paying attention. It is being fully present, wholly awake, in each moment. It is the trained ability to inhabit our own existence without remainder, so that even the simplest things—the in and out of our own breathing, the coolness of tiles on our bare feet, the way wind sculpts clouds into crocodiles and polar bears—gain the force of discovery and revelation. True attentiveness burns away the layers of indifference and ennui and distraction—all those attitudes that blend our days into a monochrome sameness—and reveals what's hidden beneath: the staggering surprise and infinite variety of every last little thing. Louis Aggasiz, Harvard's renowned biologist, returned one September to his classroom and announced to his students that he had spent the summer traveling, he had managed, he said, to get halfway across his backyard.[5] To those with eyes to see, that's enough. Everywhere we turn, wonders never cease.

One day is as good as another for practicing this kind of attentiveness. No day claims unique or superior status for the possibility of waking up. We all know people so self-absorbed and obtuse that they would miss the apocalypse if it happened in their living rooms. Their myopia is not limited to any day of the week. And we know others so alert they seem to operate in a sixth sense, deciphering the hand of God in mere whispers and flickers and shadows. Their perceptiveness is not bounded by time or circumstance.

This theme, indeed, often forms a subplot of comedy in the Bible: God or Jesus or an angelic messenger shows up, and those who should know better, *who should be paying attention*—priests, lawyers, teachers, apostles—typically miss it, while those least "deserving"—shepherds, children, beggars, whores—typically grasp it, and immediately. It turns out, numskulls are numb every day, and seekers of grace awake nearly always.

And yet, of all days we might set apart to practice the art of attentiveness, Sabbath is an outstanding candidate. Sabbath invites us to stop. In that ceasing, fresh possibilities abound. We can shut our eyes, if we choose—this is one of Sabbath's gifts, to relax without guilt. But there is also time enough to open our eyes, to learn again Jesus's command to *watch and pray*.

I recently experienced what for me was the pinnacle of the attentive life. It happened on a Tuesday, not a Sunday. But it was pure Sabbath. It was late afternoon on the Masai Mara—a wind-scoured plain cradled between the arms of two high escarpments in southern Kenya, just above Tanzania's Serengeti. The Mara is near the equator, and the crouching sun of late day spreads out in a fantail of light, creating a chiaroscuro of dazzling yellows and inky shadows. In the hour before sunset, creation pulls out all its stops: hammers light like gold flake on leaf and blade and flank, embroiders shadows dark and thick in forest and swale.

Everything stands out, as though for just this hour a fourth dimension of space has overlain the world.

Light and shadow on this day were especially strong because a storm had been gathering all afternoon. Heavy blue-black clouds rode the high ridge of Tanzania and dragged a veil of rain toward us. The immense sky was split in two above us, shimmering bright on one half, brooding dark on the other. Lightning shivered through the clouds. Thunder catapulted from them.

Our guide left the main road and slithered along a muddy, trackless field. He was driving toward a tree that stood stark and alone on the wide plain. He must have seen something out there. He was a Masai, a man who lived close to his own instincts, who sensed things long before he saw them and saw them long before anyone else did. As we neared the tree, the rest of us saw what he did: a shaggy, tawny mound that transfigured into a pride of lions. There were two leonine brothers, huge and disdainful, with a small harem of females and a den of cubs. Our guide drew close and turned off the Land Rover's motor.

The lions at first were drowsy. They lay catnapping, lolling in the warmth of the failing light. The only movement was the ruffle of wind on their manes. But then something caught the attention of one of the females. Up she sat, looked intently at whatever scent or sight had roused her, and, cool and sly, sauntered over in that direction. About a hundred feet out, she stopped, sat on her haunches, and waited. Then, one after the other, all the females and the larger cubs walked off and did the same. Each took a position about the same distance from where we'd parked, spaced twenty or thirty feet apart from one another. Then the two males stood up, stretched, and moved to opposite sides of the tree, each about fifteen feet in front of our truck.

We were, essentially, surrounded.

And then the storm hit. Against our frail encampment, rain fell, wind raged, lightning whirled, thunder broke. We zipped shut the plastic-and-canvas windows of the Land Rover, but the rain pried its way under all the unsealed places and drenched us anyway.

For the next fifteen minutes, we sat there, under siege, unable to move. We could see nothing. All we knew, and not even this for sure, was that we sat in a company of man-eaters. On a whim of hunger or anger, any one of them might rend our flimsy defenses and leave our pale bodies shredded and bloodied and strewn across the grasslands.

We had nothing to do but wait. Only *wait* is the wrong word. Waiting implies anticipation of something else: that *this* moment is not *the* moment. It implies that the expected thing, the hoped-for thing, is yet to arrive, that the present is only preliminary to the future. No, we weren't waiting, we were fully immersed in the here and now. We could not have been more present in our own lives, could not have more completely indwelt our own skins. Every sense was alive. All energy was absorbed in paying attention.

The storm passed. The lions still sat, unmoved. They had been, it turned out, no more interested in us than if we were a boulder left in the field from the last ice age.

We took one last look and carried on.

But I hope not entirely. I don't want to just carry on. I want to learn more and more to practice, here, now, always, the quality of awareness that I knew in those few minutes.

I want to learn to pass through a day without passing it by.

Yesterday it rained hard all day, a gray, sullen downpour that at times flooded windshields faster than the wipers could sweep it away, so that you had to pull over and wait for the sky to ease its anger or sorrow. But this morning dawned clean and bright. Everything glowed. I rose early. Before I lit a fire in the woodstove, I clambered onto the roof and cleaned the chimney flue, pulling a wire brisk down its length and sending plumes of soot into the crisp morning air. Then I snaked my arm into the chimney's lower cavity and scraped barnacles of creosote from it.

Then I showered. I kissed my children good-bye as they left for school. Then Cheryl and I drove to a coffee shop and got warm cinnamon buns and mugs of rich, dark coffee, and we stirred cream in until the coffee was nutty brown. We saw three friends and spoke to each. We sat in the corner, at a table strewn with sun patches, and talked at leisure about our children, about what we had read in the Bible that morning, about what the day might unfold.

Then we walked out into the bright morning. I kissed Cheryl, told her she was lovely, and set out to walk home while she took the van to do some errands. I greeted people as I went, some I knew, some I didn't. A woman in front of the train station was sweeping the maple leaves, dry as parchment, that lay in thick drifts across the pavement. I stopped and chatted with her. We both agreed the day was a gift, not to be wasted. I strode through the small town center, putting my face close to the dark windows of shops not yet open to peer inside. Near the city park I stopped to study the design of a gated arbor, thinking I might build one like it some day.

I was in no hurry. I prayed. I sang. I listened. I watched.

In all that time, I never earned a cent. I didn't write a word. I didn't build a thing. The world is no richer for my passing through it.

But I'm far richer for not missing it.

Sabbath Liturgy: Paying Attention

Loni is the office administrator at the church where I'm a pastor. Recently, she enrolled in a community college poetry class. Her motive was to enhance her already considerable skills as a songwriter, to bone up on a few tricks of diction, a ruse or two with rhyme. She went to the first class weary, wary, cranky. She resented that she'd booked herself one more night out. She had a growing skepticism that the class would be of any practical use.

Before the first night finished, she was hooked.

Two reasons: the teacher, a gifted poet himself, had an infectious love, not just for words and poems, but for life itself. He relished mystery and simplicity, the quirks of the human heart, creation's whims and flukes and feats. He was childlike with wonder, exclaiming over ordinary things that, for most of us, have become familiar to the point of invisibility.

The second reason Loni was hooked was that the class, at bedrock, was about one thing: going and doing likewise. It was about paying attention. Live with curiosity and wonder and hunger. Notice cracks in the sidewalk, the way the earth's aliveness subverts our man-made things. Notice beetles, the iridescent glaze on their hard, dark backs, their strange mix of clumsiness and agility. Notice the rubbery mottledness of a dog's nose, the fiery ribbon of a car's taillights, the way clouds one day mound thick like boulders, the next scatter thin like feathers, the next drape heavy as wet wool.

Loni rediscovered the world. She came into work the mornings after her class almost shivering with joy, eyes wide enough to swallow the sky. All things were becoming new. Here is "The Brief Fall," one of her poems that came out of her experience:

An off the cuff nudge shapes a
brief flight through the air.
The thumbtack's life now rolls in makeshift figure eight circles
as books are set on the seat to the left.
A fingernail sized spike, vital to the life of a bulletin board,
converts into a hazard
a few feet below.

Stone faced,
it lays in the comfort of the cushion in the pale green waiting room;
waiting on its prey:
adult or child,
even a toddler.
It has no conscience, no remorse.[6]

It is the simplest thing, to pay attention. But it is easily neglected. I suggest you make this a key Sabbath Liturgy, a wide bridge you build to cross from your life now—which, if it bears any resemblance to what mine can be, is marked by frantic busyness and chronic distraction—to a life of restfulness and wonder.

Have you ever written a poem? Poetry is the first art form, the primal, almost instinctual way humans try to reflect and make sense of the world's bigness and wildness and danger and beauty. Failing that, our next reflex is just to box up the world, to categorize and file it. One writer was asked when he first became a poet, and he answered something like this: "I think we are all born with a natural desire to discover and create. We're all born poets. The real question is, when did you stop being one?"

Why not return to it right now? Why not write a poem?

Stop. Look. Look close.

Notice the sun falling slantwise through the window, the dust's slow dance in it. Or touch the threadbare edges of your chair's upholstery, and remember that day it arrived new, smelling synthetic, clashing a bit with the paint on the walls. Ah, now look at the intricate folds of your child's ear, the way light bleeds through the thin, taut flesh of it. Gaze outside and see the wind spin larch leaves like fish lures. Watch the darkness sift down the hillside and gather in the fir boughs.

See it all. Like Adam, name it.

Resolve to live this way more often.

FOUR

IN GOD'S TIME:
Stopping to See God's Bigness

One day the windows in our house started to rattle, all at once. Dishes clinked and pinged in the cupboards. Ornaments fell off the mantel. The floor turned semigelatinous.

Then it stopped.

It was an earthquake. Tectonic plates nearby nudged each other in passing, bumped shoulders. The resulting shudder wasn't brusque enough to do structural damage—it didn't splinter joists, sheer pipes, or shatter glass. It just pulled a few pranks.

We picked up the fallen ornaments, inspected them for chips and cracks. We opened the cupboards—cautiously—and set bowls and cups and glasses back on their bases. We straightened pictures that had slipped askew. We checked the water pipes where they join the house. We would have checked the gas line, too, except we don't have one.

No big deal.

But it makes you slightly edgy, living here, above what seismologists tell you are many ragged seams loosely stitched, many raw scars badly sutured, many fractured bones hastily set and splinted. They say we're due, overdue, for a real shakedown, a great hullabaloo of seismic vengeance that would swallow coastlines and resculpt mountain ranges and make the ocean stack up on itself catastrophically. We can't do anything about that, except move, and we don't want to.

But we can get ready. We keep in our shed many gallons of water, held in rinsed-out milk cartons and purified with a few drops of iodine. They wait for that day when the shift beneath the earth's crust is violent enough to sever water pipes, perhaps disruptive enough to infuse poison gases into our nearby rivers and streams. As well, the schools routinely drill our children on earthquake survival skills: stand back from windows and mirrors, anything that might fall like blades, get out from beneath heavy objects that might twist loose and plummet, crawl under a sturdy table that's unlikely to buckle. Wait it out.

Expect aftershocks.

Watch your step afterward.

Be careful opening doors and cupboards.

Above all, don't panic. Panic will wipe out everything else you know.

It's an odd way to look at it, but Sabbath is preparedness training of sorts. It gets us ready for a time, a time we can anticipate but can't predict, when the world as we know it will fall to pieces. It trains us in practical wisdom, clear judgment, skillful response. It slows us down enough to notice what truly matters.

The most moving stories of the Jewish people keeping Sabbath are the ones when they kept it in the midst of crisis and terror. They kept Sabbath under siege. They kept it in famine. They kept it in drought. They kept it in Warsaw's ghettos and Hitler's death camps and Stalin's gulags. They kept Sabbath when the world was falling to pieces.

Their keeping it in their days of peace and abundance and freedom prepared them for keeping it in times of war and scarcity and captivity. Their keeping it nurtured something deep and hidden in them that came to light only on the day of testing.

As the rabbis are fond of saying, more than Israel ever kept the Sabbath, the Sabbath kept Israel. I would alter this slightly: *to the extent* that they kept Sabbath, Sabbath kept them. Sabbath living orients us toward that which, apart from rest, we will always miss.

The root idea of Sabbath is simple as rain falling, basic as breathing. It's that all living things—and many nonliving things too—thrive only by an ample measure of stillness. A bird flying, never nesting, is soon plummeting. Grass trampled, day after day, scalps down to the hard bone of earth. Fruit constantly inspected bruises, blights. This is true of other things as well: a saw used without relenting—its teeth never filed, its blade never cooled—grows dull and brittle; a motor never shut off gums with residue or fatigues from thinness of oil—it sputters, it stalls, it seizes. Even companionship languishes without seasons of apartness.

God stitched into the nature of things an inviolable need to be left alone now and then. The primary way people receive this aloneness and stillness is, of course, through sleep. We can defy slumber only so long—propping ourselves upright with caffeine, manufacturing artificial alertness with drugs—but past a certain point, we collapse. We must submit to sleep's benign tyranny, enter its inescapable vulnerability and solitariness (in sleep we're easily besieged or abandoned, and we are by ourselves even when enwrapped by another's arms). Unless we do, we die.

Not long ago I tried to outrun my limits. I was preparing to go away and so crammed my last few working days precariously full, like a bus in Delhi. I was up hours before dawn, answering e-mails, finishing reports, speed-reading correspondence, tossing back responses. Then off to a breakfast meeting, and from there into a day of troubleshooting, firefighting, strategy planning, troop rallying, complaint management. A working lunch. More appointments, deadlines, negotiations, each segment as intricately fitted to others as the parts of a circuit board. A quick dinner with the family. Back to a meeting that deadlocked in niggling details. Home about midnight. Only to get up the next day, after lying awake half the night thinking about all the things I had failed in or forgotten to do, and repeat a slight variation of the same thing. In the midst of that, I sat down in my study to read something or write something—ask me what, even at gunpoint or with the promise of vast wealth set before me, and I couldn't tell you. And I collapsed. I fell into a sleep so deep that, had God plucked a rib from my side, fashioned a woman from it, and brought her to me naked, I wouldn't have so much as twitched. The office administrator came by to ask me something, saw me, watched to make sure I was breathing, and went and fetched my assistant, and the two stood in the doorway, laughing.

I was oblivious. I was far, far away—in the darkness of Sheol, in the brightness of seventh heaven, who knows? My body had been pushed and bullied, cajoled and coerced long enough, it staged a general strike, an all-out boycott. I had lost the power to resist.

I slept.

The tricky thing about Sabbath, though, is it's a form of rest unlike sleep. Sleep is so needed that, defied too long, our bodies inevitably, even violently, force the issue. Sleep eventually waylays all fugitives. It catches you and has its way with you.

Sabbath won't do that. Resisted, it backs off. Spurned, it flees. It's easy to skirt or defy Sabbath, to manufacture cheap substitutes in its place—and to do all that, initially, without noticeable damage, and sometimes, briefly, with admirable results. It's easy, in other words, to spend most of your life breaking Sabbath and never figure out that this is part of the reason your work's unsatisfying, your friendships patchy, your leisure threadbare, your vacations exhausting.

We simply haven't taken time. We've not been still long enough, often enough, to know ourselves, our friends, our family. Our God. Indeed, the worst hallucination busyness conjures is the conviction that *I am* God. *All depends on me. How will the right things happen at the right time if I'm not pushing and pulling and watching and worrying?*

Sabbath-keeping requires two orientations. One is Godward.

The other is timeward. To keep Sabbath well—as both a day and an attitude—we have to think clearly about God and freshly about time. We likely, at some level, need to change our minds about both. Unless we trust God's sovereignty, we won't dare risk Sabbath. And unless we receive time as abundance and gift, not as ration and burden, we'll never develop a capacity to savor Sabbath.

So let's talk about both, first the Godward orientation, and then the timeward one.

First, God.

Jewish Sabbath begins in the evening. It begins, in other words, with sleep. Sleep, I already said, is a necessity. But it is also a relinquishment. It is self-abandonment: of control, of power, of consciousness, of identity. We direct nothing in our sleep. We master nothing. We lose ourselves and are carried like children or prisoners into a netherworld alternately grotesque and idyllic, carnivalesque and elysian. In sleep we become infants again: utterly vulnerable, completely defenseless, totally dependent. Out of control. I knew a man, a hard-fisted, burly man who could snap your bones like sticks with his bare hands, whose house was burglarized while he slept a mere arm's length from the prowler. He knew nothing of it until morning. His girth and brawn may as well have been a baby's downy softness for all the good it did him.

So sleep, besides being a necessity, is also an act of faith. "O LORD, how many are my foes! / How many rise up against me!" David begins Psalm 3. But then he declares: *"I lie down and sleep; / I wake again, because the LORD sustains me"* (vv. 1, 5, emphasis mine). Or the next psalm: *"I will lie down and sleep in peace, / for you alone, O LORD, / make me dwell in safety"* (Ps. 4:8, emphasis mine). Every time we sleep we place ourselves again in this position of vulnerability, of defenselessness, of dependency. We enter again this infantlike unguardedness. And we do this well only under one of two conditions: utter exhaustion, where we can't help ourselves, or complete confidence, where we stop trying to help ourselves. Then we sleep because we know from whence our help comes. We sleep because we know in whom we have believed and are confident that he is able to keep that which we have entrusted to him. We give ourselves, regardless of our unfinished business, into God's care. We sleep simply because we believe God will look after us.

It's the same with Sabbath rest. Real Sabbath, the kind that empties and fills us, depends on the second condition, on complete confidence and trust. And confidence and trust like that are rooted in a deep conviction that God is good and God is sovereign.

There's no rest for those who don't believe that. If God works all things together for good for those who love him and are called to his purposes, you can relax. If he doesn't, start worrying. If God can take any mess, any mishap, any wastage, any wreckage, any anything, and choreograph beauty and meaning from it, then you can take a day off. If he can't, get busy. Either God's always at work, watching the city, building the house, or you need to try harder.

Either God is good and in control, or it all depends on you.

Sietze Buning's poem "Obedience" is a quiet meditation on the surprising fruit such trust in God can bear in time.

> Were my parents right or wrong
> not to mow the ripe oats that Sunday morning
> with the rainstorm threatening?
>
> I reminded them that the Sabbath was made
> for man
> and of the ox fallen into the pit.
> Without an oats crop, I argued,
> the cattle would need to survive on town-
> bought oats
> and then it wouldn't pay to keep them.
> Isn't selling cattle at a loss like an ox in a pit?

The Rest of God

My parents did not argue.
We went to church.
We sang the usual psalms louder than usual—
we, and the others whose harvests were at stake:

"Jerusalem, where blessing waits
Our feet are standing in thy gates.
God, be merciful to me;
On thy grace I rest my plea."

Dominie made no concession on sermon length:

"Five Good Reasons for Infant Baptism,"
    though we heard little of it,
    for more floods came and winds blew and beat
    upon the House than we had figured on, even,
    more lightning and thunder
    and hail the size of pullet eggs.
Falling branches snapped the electric wires.
We sang the closing psalm without the organ
    and in the dark:

"Ye seed from Abraham descended,
God's covenant love is never ended."

Afterward we rode by our oats field, flattened.

"We still mow it," Dad said.
"Ten bushels to the acre, maybe, what would have been fifty
    if I had mowed right after milking
    and if the whole family had shocked.
We could have had it weatherproof before the storm."

Later at dinner Dad said,
"God was testing us. I'm glad we went."
"Those psalms never gave me such a lift as this morning,"
Mother said, "I wouldn't have missed it."
And even I thought but did not say,
how guilty we would feel now if we had saved the harvest.
The one time Dad asked me why I live in a
black neighborhood,
I reminded him of that Sunday morning.
Immediately he understood.[1]

King David's a good model for depth of trust. That man trusted in God's goodness and sovereignty. The evidence is laced throughout his "diary," the psalms he wrote. Psalm 62 is a good example. It begins with a declaration: "My soul finds rest in God alone; / my salvation comes from him. / He alone is my rock and my salvation; / he is my fortress, I will never be shaken" (vv. 1–2).

David is training himself—and whoever else will listen—in God's sovereignty. This is for him no mere intellectual exercise, but a way of survival. It is the shape of his life in the holy wild. The context of the psalm is distress: David is beset by enemies bent on his ruin, adversaries who cloak malice with flattery, who "with their mouths . . . bless, / but in their hearts . . . curse" (v. 4). The only way to truly rest in a world like that—a world of deceit and enmity—is to "find rest in God alone." David had no way to dredge up rest from his circumstances. It had to be sought elsewhere. It had to come from God. David had to know God as his rock, his salvation, his unshakable fortress: that God alone is sovereign and works all things together for good for those who love him and are called to his purposes.

But notice something, because it helps us to train ourselves likewise. David starts with declaration—a confident assertion that his soul finds rest in God alone. But he shifts tone slightly yet significantly at verse 5. He virtually repeats verbatim what he says at the opening, but watch for the change: "Find rest, O my soul, in God alone; / my hope comes from him. / He alone is my rock and my salvation; / he is my fortress, I will not be shaken" (vv. 5–6).

David moves from declaration to imperative. He moves from saying how it is to saying how it ought to be, from celebration to exhortation, from a diary of experience to a manual of instruction. This even takes on a liturgical shape, where David in the middle of the psalm steps back from personal reflection and testimony and speaks to the congregation: "Trust in him at all times, O people; / pour out your hearts to him, / for God is our refuge" (v. 8).

I like the honesty and practicality of this. I waver between these two things—my experience of God's sovereignty and my need to take hold of it afresh. One minute I'm declaring that *I do* rest in him, the next exhorting myself that *I can.* And the exhortation moves the inside to the outside, from myself to the congregation, from testimony to liturgy—*trust in him at all times, O people.*

In *Prince Caspian*, part of C. S. Lewis's Narnia Chronicles, the children Peter, Susan, Edmund, and Lucy all find themselves in Narnia after a long absence. Aslan, the great king and lion, is nowhere to be seen. Lucy, the youngest of the children, particularly aches to see him. One night she wakes to a great stirring in the forest, and to a voice calling her. While the other children sleep, she ventures forth through the woods and into a clearing. Here's what happens:

> A circle of grass, smooth as a lawn, met her eyes, with dark trees dancing all round it. And then—oh joy! For *he* was there: the huge Lion, shining white in the moonlight, with his huge black shadow underneath him.
>
> But for the movement of his tail he might have been a stone lion, but Lucy never thought of that. She never stopped to think whether he was a friendly lion or not. She rushed to him. She felt her heart would burst if she lost a moment. And the next thing she knew was that she was kissing him and put-

> ting her arms as far round his neck as she could and burying her face in the beautiful rich silkiness of his mane.
>
> "Aslan, Aslan. Dear Aslan," sobbed Lucy. "At last."
>
> The great beast rolled over on his side so that Lucy fell, half sitting and half lying between his front paws. He bent forward and just touched her nose with his tongue. His warm breath came all round her. She gazed up into the large wise face.
>
> "Welcome, child," he said.
>
> "Aslan," said Lucy, "you're bigger."
>
> "That is because you are older, little one," answered he.
>
> "Not because you are?"
>
> "I am not. But every year you grow, you will find me bigger."[2]

That's a perfect description of those who train themselves in God's goodness and sovereignty: every year you grow, you find him bigger.

The best way I know to embody this Godward orientation is thankfulness. Thankfulness is a secret passageway into a room you can't find any other way. It is the wardrobe into Narnia. It allows us to discover the rest of God—those dimensions of God's world, God's presence, God's character that are hidden, always, from the thankless. Ingratitude is an eye disease every bit as much as a heart disease. It sees only flaws, scars, scarcity. Likewise, the god of the thankless is wary, stingy, grudging, bumbling, nitpicky. He's by turns meddlesome and apathetic, suspicious then indifferent, grubbing about in our domestic trifles one moment, oblivious to our personal catastrophes the next.

But to give thanks, to render it as Scripture tells us we ought—in all circumstances, for all things, to the glory of God—such thanksgiving becomes a declaration of God's sovereign goodness. Even more, it trains us in a growing awareness of that sovereign goodness. You cannot practice thankfulness on a biblical scale without its altering the way you see. And the more you do it, the more you find cause for doing it. Inherent in a life of thanksgiving is an ongoing discovery of God's sufficiency, his generosity, his fatherly affection and warrior protection. "To the faithful," David said of God, "you show yourself faithful" (2 Sam. 22:26).

In Guelph, Ontario, there's a riverside park landmarked with large and intricate sculptures: a dinosaur, a man riding a bicycle, a child and his mother. But these are no ordinary sculptures. Each is made from the debris collected from the riverbed. Every year, the city drains the river by a system of channel locks, then invites people from the community to scour the river's muddy floor and clean up the garbage scattered along it. A welter of refuse is dredged up: shopping carts, tires and rims, car hoods, baby strollers, bikes and trikes, engine blocks, rakes and shovels, urinals, copper plumbing, wine bottles, shoes, thousands of pop cans. Mountains and mountains of rust-scabbed rubbish, slick with algae, are hauled out. Rather than truck all this garbage off to a landfill, the city calls its sculptors together (though most of the pop cans are turned in for refund and the money donated to park conservation). Each artist is given a mound of junk and commissioned to make from it beauty. The created works are then showcased along the very river from which the raw materials have come.

God does that. He works all things together for good for those who love him and are called to his purposes. He takes junk and sculpts art.

And the primary way we participate in that is thanksgiving. Be thankful in all things. Be thankful for all things.

Like the apostle Paul.

One day Paul and Silas were in Philippi, in Macedonia, in what today is northern Greece. The two friends were going to "the place of prayer" (Acts 16:16). The first time they went there, they met Lydia, a local businesswoman, and led her to faith in Christ (see Acts 16:11–15). She would later become a key leader in the Philippian church. This time, a slave girl with a "foreign" spirit meets them on the way. The girl has been a jackpot for her owners. The spirit in her shows her things, hidden things, future things. Her owners exploit her as a soothsayer and fortune-teller. They've grown rich off her captivity. When the girl spots Paul and Silas, her sixth sense kicks in, and she follows them around, shouting, "These men are servants of the Most High God, who are telling you the way to be saved" (Acts 16:17).

This is good marketing. A girl, already widely sought for her "spiritual" insights, to whom many in the city ascribe supernatural powers, now broadcasts, at no charge and with approval, the evangelists' identity and work. It's like some syndicated horoscope columnist advising people to listen to Franklin Graham. Why quibble with that? If Paul was the least inclined to exploit the slave girl—everyone else does—he might have kept mum.

But Paul cares more about the girl than he does his own advertising campaign. He cares more about her freedom than his own success. He cares more about her coming to know the Most High God herself, finding the way to be saved, than about her telling others about such things while she remains on the outside.

So Paul turns and casts the spirit out of her.

And then, as is often the case, when heaven breaks in, all hell breaks loose.

The girl's owners are furious. Their "hope of making money was gone" (Acts 16:19). This gospel stuff can be bad for local industry and economy. They seize Paul and Silas, haul them before the city magistrates, and there create a ruckus. The magistrates have Paul and Silas stripped and beaten and handed over to the jailer, who places them in a cell within a cell and shackles their feet for good measure.

And there they sit, in the cramped gloom of the prison house. Cold metal bites their raw flesh. Its weight presses on their throbbing muscles and aching bones. Blood fills their mouths with a coppery taste. Bruises bloom like dark flowers on their backs, swell like tumors on their faces. The fetid air of the cell breeds infection in their open cuts. Blood thickens around their wounds.

This is their reward for doing good, for loving the least of these.

What would you do? Curse, moan, demand? What would you feel? Anger, self-pity, terror? Would you nurse thoughts of vengeance?

Paul and Silas sing. Paul and Silas pray. Paul and Silas hold church. They take Sabbath. They rejoice in the suffering. They consider it pure joy to go through trials of many kinds. They worship the God who can make art from junk.

And all the while, both prison guard and prisoners listen.

Then a miracle happens. An earthquake hits, of such magnitude that the chains fall off the prisoners, all of them, and the cell doors fly open, each of them.

But that's not the miracle. This is: just as the jailer who tossed Paul and Silas into the inner cell, who clamped the chains on their ankles—just as he is about to kill himself because he thinks all his prisoners have escaped, a voice rings out from the shadows: "Don't harm yourself! We're all here!" (see Acts 16:28).

It's Paul shouting.

We're all here?

I can understand that Paul and Silas would stay. I can understand that they would refuse to seize an opportunity for their own advantage if it involved another's loss. They already showed that spirit with the slave girl.

But who's *we*? Who else has refused to seize this opportunity, to grab freedom through this one narrow window suddenly opened, soon to shut?

Who's *we*? It's the other prisoners. It's those who sat and listened to two men singing in the rain, singing in their pain, praying in their agony—two men who didn't succumb to the voice of complaint but instead raised the voice of thanksgiving.

Who's *we*? It's all those who, before this instant, never imagined thankfulness as a possible response to life's hardships and injustices. It's all those who, until this moment, could not conceive of a God so good and so present that he is able to conjure good from evil. It's all those who are surprised to find, right here in the pit, a God sovereign enough that those who place themselves under his care consider it pure joy when they go through trials of many kinds.

We are all those who discover, this very night, a God worthy to be praised in all things and for all things.

We're all here.

The Philippian jailer rushes up to Paul and Silas with one question: "What must I do to be saved?" (Acts 16:30). *What must I do to meet the God you know, the God whose love inspires thankfulness no matter what, the God who can subdue the hardest heart, the God who can put into the hearts of captives compassion for their captor?*

Of course they're all here. They have just found the God who sets prisoner and prison guard free. The God who makes art from junk.

Where else would they go?

That's the first orientation for good Sabbath-keeping, the Godward one. It is to practice, mostly through thankfulness, the presence of God until you are utterly convinced of his goodness and sovereignty, until he's bigger, and you find your rest in him alone.

Sabbath Liturgy: Practicing the Sovereignty of God

One thing stops God dead in his tracks. It is paltry and flimsy, but tenacious enough to shatter all God's advances. Even grace, abounding in our sin, cannot break it.

I speak of pride.

Pride usurps God. Pride inverts the universe's deepest truth: that we need and serve God. Pride gets this exactly backward. Pride is the delusion that God, if he exists, is awfully lucky I've shown up and should mind his p's and q's lest I change my mind.

The twin of pride is despair. It is to collapse into a sense that not even God is good enough or big enough or smart enough to sort out the mess I've made or stumbled upon. In despair, we are consumed by the lie that God, if he exists, is too inept or distracted or apathetic to even notice us, let alone come to our aid.

Judas was a man who went from one to the other, pride to despair, in a blink. His betrayal of Jesus is an act of unmitigated pridefulness, the swaggering assurance that he knew what was best and had every right—even a moral imperative—to go after it. He was cocksure in his actions, driven by a sense of higher wisdom. But that quickly fell to pieces, and then Judas acted out of utmost remorse. No one and nothing, he felt, could salvage his blunder. The only thing left to do was hang himself.

Judas represents an extreme, but the pattern itself is commonplace: one minute certain we can do things better than God, the next convinced that not even God can make things better. Peter, who is often contrasted with Judas, was like that. Boastful and bullheaded, given to brags and bullyrags, he promised great feats, committed great blunders, and then slunk away in defeat. He crowed with cocky self-admiration, and then, hearing the cock crow, wept with shameful humiliation.

But eventually he got it right. And his secret, as far as he had one, was that he learned to practice the sovereignty of God.

Acts 3–4, for instance. Peter and John perform a miracle in Jerusalem, and then Peter seizes the opportunity to preach one of his shoot-from-the-hip, come-to-Jesus sermons. This lands them in trouble with the "law," the Jewish high council known as the Sanhedrin. Peter seizes that opportunity to preach at them. They are astonished at his courage. He is one who speaks with authority.

But they order him and John to shut up about Jesus anyway, "to speak no longer to anyone in this name" (Acts 4:17)—a rather comprehensive prohibition. They threaten Peter and John with dire consequences if they persist.

The Peter we knew before would have folded long before this point. He would have wormed his way out, found some escape hatch, and slipped through it. The Peter we meet now is emboldened by each fresh challenge. The Sanhedrin note this: "When they saw the courage of Peter and John and realized that they were unschooled, ordinary men, they were astonished and they took note that these men had been with Jesus" (Acts 4:13). Confidence in ourselves—our educations, our pedigrees, our abilities—is pathetic. But confidence in Jesus Christ, which comes only by walking with him, is astonishing. Peter has quit the one and perfected the other.

It's what happens next, after the Sanhedrin release John and Peter, that gives us the clearest account of how Peter replenishes his Christ-confidence:

> On their release, Peter and John went back to their own people and reported all that the chief priests and elders had said to them. When they heard this, they raised their voices together in prayer to God. "Sovereign Lord," they said, "you made the heaven and the earth and the sea, and everything in them. You spoke by the Holy Spirit through the mouth of your servant, our father David:

> "'Why do the nations rage and the peoples plot in vain? The kings of the earth take their stand and the rulers gather together against the Lord and against his Anointed One.'
>
> Indeed Herod and Pontius Pilate met together with the Gentiles and the people of Israel in this city to conspire against your holy servant Jesus, whom you anointed. They did what your power and will had decided beforehand should happen. Now, Lord, consider their threats and enable your servants to speak your word with great boldness. Stretch out your hand to heal and perform miraculous signs and wonders through the name of your holy servant Jesus."
>
> After they prayed, the place where they were meeting was shaken. And they were all filled with the Holy Spirit and spoke the word of God boldly. (Acts 4:23–31)

The prayer ends with the trouble these men face. But it doesn't begin this way. It begins with this: "Sovereign Lord." And it moves from there into naming and recounting the height and depth and weight of his sovereignty: God made all, rules all, and overrules all that stands in his way.

These men practice the sovereignty of God. They establish, clear and solid, the truth of God's kingship. They rehearse the reality of God's overarching, undergirding might. As they grow, God starts to look bigger.

And only then, as a kind of addendum or footnote, do they pray about the problem they have: *Oh, by the way, God: we had some trouble in town today, some blowhards making empty threats. Could you clear it up?*

God then sends a fresh infusion of the Spirit. They grow some more. God sends his Spirit, but not to keep the disciples safe: to make them more dangerous.

Are you in the midst of a situation where, as you pray, you find yourself putting the problem first? If so, you're starting where you should end. You're rehearsing the problem, making it seem larger than it is, when what you need to do is rehearse God's greatness and bigness. Then the problem shrinks to its right portions. *Oh, by the way . . .*

As a Sabbath Liturgy, I recommend practicing the sovereignty of God. Today when you pray, start with God. Survey what he has made. Recite what he has done. Proclaim who he is.

And after you have been with Jesus long enough, and feel your courage brimming, and he looks bigger, see if there's still an *Oh, by the way . . .*

FIVE

The Rest of Time: *Stopping to Number Our Days Aright*

Sabbath-keeping is more than time management. It is a fresh orientation to time, where we think with holy imagination about how the arc of our moments and hours and days intersects with eternity. "Teach us to number our days aright," Moses asked God, "that we may gain a heart of wisdom" (Ps. 90:12). *Teach us that this is not just another day of the week, but the day that the Lord has made.*

This is God's time-management technique. There's a right way to tally up days. There's an arithmetic of timekeeping, and God must tutor us in it. Wisdom is not the precondition for learning this arithmetic. It's the fruit of it. Wisdom comes from learning to number our days aright. You don't need to be wise to sign up for God's school. But if you're diligent, attentive, inquisitive in his classes, you'll emerge that way.

It's easy to get this wrong. God's school is not like most. It's not regimented, age-adjusted, fixed in its curriculum. The classroom is life itself, the curriculum all life's demands and interruptions and tedium, its surprises and disappointments. In the midst of this, through these things themselves, God hands us an abacus and tells us to tally it all up.

Meaning?

Meaning, work out where time and eternity meet. Pay attention to how God is afoot in the mystery of each moment, in its mad rush or maddening plod. He is present in all that. But too often we are so time-obsessed we take no time to really notice. I have a pastor friend in Toronto who one day after a Sunday service received a note: "Pastor Peter, I would appreciate it if you prayed shorter prayers. Your pastoral prayer this past Sunday was twelve minutes, forty-three seconds in length. Please strive for greater brevity."

The note was unsigned. The only thing we know about this man, this woman, this child, is that the writer is so bound in time—counting the minutes—that he or she has never learned to number his or her days. This person can tell time but not discern seasons.

But miss that, and you miss wisdom. For only those who number their days aright gain wise hearts. Only they become God's sages: those calm, unhurried people who live in each moment fully, savoring simple things, celebrating small epiphanies, unafraid of life's inevitable surprises and reverses, adaptive to change yet not chasing after it.

Able to pray with those who pray.

I write this at a time when the church talks much about being purpose-driven. This is a good thing, but we ought to practice a bit of holy cynicism about it. We should be a little uneasy about the pairing of purposefulness with drivenness. Something's out of kilter there. Drivenness may awaken or be a catalyst for purpose, but it rarely fulfills it, more often it jettisons it. A common characteristic of driven people is that, at some point, they forget the purpose. They lose the point. The very reason they began something—embarked on a journey, undertook a project, waged a war, entered a profession, married a girl—erodes under the weight of their striving. Their original inspiration may be noble. But driven too hard, it gets supplanted by greed for more, or dread of setback, or force of habit.

Drivenness erodes purposefulness.

The difference between living on purpose and being driven surfaces most clearly in what we do with time. The driven are fanatical time managers—time mongers, time herders, time hoarders. Living on purpose requires skillful time management, true, but not the kind that turns brittle, that attempts to quarantine most of what makes life itself—the mess, the surprise, the breakdowns, the breakthroughs. Too much rigidity stifles purpose. I find that the more I try to manage time, the more anxious I get about it.

And the more prone I am to lose my purpose.

The truly purposeful have an ironic secret: they manage time less and pay attention more. The most purposeful people I know rarely overmanage time, and when they do it's usually because they're lapsing into drivenness, into a loss of purpose for which they overcompensate with mere busyness. No, the distinguishing mark of the purposeful is not time management.

It's that they *notice*. They're fully awake.

Jesus, for example. He lived life with the clearest and highest purpose. Yet he veered and strayed from one interruption to the next, with no apparent plan in hand other than his single, overarching one: get to Jerusalem and die. Otherwise, his days, as far as we can figure, were a series of zigzags and detours, apparent whims and second thoughts, interruptions and delays, off-the-cuff plans, spur-of-the-moment decisions, leisurely meals, serendipitous rounds of storytelling.

Who touched me?

You give them something to eat.

Let's go to the other side.

Jesus was available—or not—according to some oblique logic all his own. He had an inner ear for the Father's whispers, a third eye for the Spirit's motions. One minute he's not going to the temple, the next he is. One minute he refuses to help a wedding host solve his wine drought, the next he's all over it. He's ready to drop everything and rush over to a complete stranger's house to heal his servant but dawdles four days while Lazarus—"the one he loves"—writhes in his death throes (see John 11:3); or fails to come at all when John—"the greatest in the kingdom of heaven"—languishes on death row (see Matt.

11:1–11). The closest we get to what dictated Jesus's schedule is his own statement in John's Gospel: "The wind blows wherever it pleases. You hear its sound, but you cannot tell where it comes from or where it is going. So it is with everyone born of the Spirit" (John 3:8).

The apostle Peter, after declaring that Jesus is "Lord of all," describes the supreme Sovereign's modus operandi: "God anointed Jesus of Nazareth with the Holy Spirit and power, *and . . . he went around doing good*" (Acts 10:36, 38, emphasis mine). So that's it, the sum of Christ's earthly vocation: he wandered and he blessed. He was a physician vagabond. He was the original doctor without borders. His purpose was crystallized, but his method almost scattershot. "My whole life I have been complaining that my work was constantly interrupted," Henri Nouwen said near the end of his life, "until I discovered the interruptions were my work."[1]

No, Jesus didn't seem to keep time. But he *noticed.* So many people along the way—blind men, lame men, wild men, fishermen, tax men, weeping whores, pleading fathers, grieving mothers, dying children, singing children, *anyone*—captured his attention. He stopped to tell a lot of stories, many of which arose out of, well, more interruptions: "Teacher, tell my brother to divide the inheritance with me" (Luke 12:13); "Teacher, what must I do to inherit eternal life?" (Luke 10:25); "Son of David, have mercy on me!" (Matt. 15:22). What's more, he invited others to go and do likewise. Those driven to get and spend, to judge and exclude, he called to attention.

Look at the birds!
Look at those flowers!
Do you see this woman?
Where are the other nine?
Why do you call me good?
Who do you say I am?

Life does not consist of the abundance of our possessions, Jesus warned. And then he told a story about a rich fool who noticed all the trivial things and was oblivious to all the important ones. What matters, Jesus concluded, isn't being rich in stuff, it's being rich toward God. He explained the essence of such richness elsewhere: it's having eyes to see, ears to hear.

It's to notice, to pay attention to the time of God's visitation.

"The dream of my life," Mary Oliver writes,

> Is to lie down by a slow river
> And stare at the light in the trees—
> To learn something of being nothing
> A little while but the rich
> Lens of attention.[2]

Jesus was that "rich lens of attention."

To live on purpose means to go and do likewise. Purposefulness requires paying attention, and paying attention means—almost by definition—that we make room for surprise. We become hospitable to interruption. I doubt we can *notice* for long without this hospitality. And to sustain it we need theological touchstones for it—a conviction in our bones that God is Lord of our days and years, and that *his* purposes and his presence often come disguised as detours, messes, defeats.

I came to you naked, Jesus says. *I came to you thirsty.*

"When, Lord?" we ask, startled.

When he wore the disguise of an interruption.

Think a moment of all the events and encounters that have shaped you most deeply and lastingly. How many did you see coming? How many did you engineer, manufacture, chase down?

And how many were interruptions?

Children? You might have planned as meticulously as a NASA rocket launch, but did you have any idea, really, what it would be like, who this child in your arms really was, who you would become because of him or her? The span between life as we intend it and life as we receive it is vast. Our true purpose is worked out in that gap. It is fashioned in the crucible of interruptions.

Mr. Holland's Opus is the story of a man with a magnificent ambition. He wants to be a great composer. But he still has to pay the bills, so he and his young wife move to a small town where he teaches high school music, strictly for the money. All the while, he works on his masterpiece, his opus, laying the ground for his real calling. The plan is to teach for a few years, then step into his destiny.

But life keeps intruding. One year folds into two, into five, into fifteen. And then one day, Mr. Holland is old, and the school board shuffles him out for early retirement. He packs his desk. His wife and grown son come to fetch him. Walking down the school's wide, empty hallways, he hears a sound in the auditorium. He goes to see what it is.

It's a surprise.

Hundreds of his students from his years of teaching—many now old themselves—dozens of his colleagues, both current and former, hundreds of friends, fans, well-wishers, the room is packed. All have gathered to say thank you. An orchestra is there, made up of Mr. Holland's students through the years. They've been preparing to perform Mr. Holland's opus—the composition that, over four decades, he hammered out and tinkered with, polished, discarded, recovered, reworked, never finished.

They play it now.

But, of course, he knows, everyone knows: his opus isn't the composition. His real opus, his true life's masterpiece, stands before him, here, now. It's not the music. It is all these lives—men and women, young and old—his life has touched. It is all these people his passions and convictions have helped and shaped. It's all that's being formed in the crucible of interruptions.

This is his work. This is his purpose.

Finally, after all these years, he's learned to number his days.

In 1973, the comedian Johnny Carson nearly caused a national crisis with a single wisecrack. That was the year North America's long flight of postwar prosperity fell to earth like a shot goose in one ungainly plummet. There was runaway inflation. There were oil and food shortages. All the abundance that Americans had come to see as their due, their birthright, suddenly seemed in jeopardy.

And so on December 19, 1973, at 11:35 p.m., when Johnny Carson walked on the live studio set of *The Tonight Show* and quipped, "There's an acute shortage of toilet paper in the United States," it wasn't funny. The joke had a toehold in reality: earlier in the day, Congressman Harold Froehlich from Wisconsin had warned that if the federal bureaucracy didn't get its act together soon and catch up on its supply bids, government agencies would run out of toilet tissue within a month or two. Carson took this shard of trivia and played it for a laugh. Then, as was his trademark, he swung at an invisible golf ball, took a commercial break, and got on with the show.

Not so the nation. Twenty million viewers flew into panic. The next morning, hundreds of thousands of frantic shoppers lined up outside the supermarkets of America, poised to dash to the paper aisles and stockpile rolls, fighting over bundles of two-ply and four-ply. There were brawls in aisleways and scrums at the checkout. Some store managers tried to limit sales—four rolls per customer—but they had no way of monitoring how many times a customer came back, and most came back repeatedly. By noon on December 20—mere hours after Johnny's flippant remark—America was sold out. "I never saw anything like it," one dazed grocer in New Jersey said.[3]

Johnny Carson's one offhand gag line had sparked a national run on toilet tissue.

We're generally gullible about news of scarcity. We have, it seems, an inbuilt skittishness about shortfall. This has been with us a long while, since the garden, by my reckoning.

Most of us live afraid that we're almost out of time. But you and I, we're heirs of eternity. We're not short of days.

We just need to number them aright.

Sabbath Liturgy: Redeeming the Time

"The world of the generous," Eugene Peterson translates Proverbs 11:24, "gets larger and larger; / the world of the stingy gets smaller and smaller" (MSG). This is more than a principle of financial stewardship, it's a basic truth of life. Generous people *generate* things. And, consequently, their worlds are more varied, surprising, colorful, fruitful. They're richer. More abounds with them, and yet they have a greater thirst and deeper capacity to take it all in. The world delights the generous but seldom overwhelms them.

Not so the stingy. Stinginess is parasitic, it chews life up and spits out bones. The stingy end up losing what they try so desperately to hold. As Jesus warned, those who store up treasure only on earth discover, too late, that such storage is merely composting. Or, as he warned in the parable of the talents, trying to preserve a thing intact never accomplishes even that much. Hoarding is only wasting. Keeping turns into losing. And so the world of the stingy shrinks. Skinflints, locked into a mind-set of scarcity, find that the world dwindles down to meet their withered expectations. Because they are convinced there isn't enough, there never is.

This all relates to Sabbath-keeping. Generous people have more time. That's the irony: those who sanctify time and who give time away—who treat time as gift and not possession—have time in abundance. Contrariwise, those who guard every minute, resent every interruption, ration every moment, never have enough. They're always late, always behind, always scrambling, always driven. There is, of course, a place for wise management of our days and weeks and years. But management can quickly turn into rigidity. We hold time so tight we crush it, like a flower closed in the fist. We thought we were protecting it, but all we did was destroy it.

The taproot of generosity is spiritual. The apostle Paul, when he explains to the Corinthians about the astounding generosity of the Macedonians, remarks, "They gave themselves *first to the Lord* and then to us" (2 Cor. 8:5, emphasis mine). True generosity always moves in that sequence: first God, then others. First the Spirit, then the flesh.

And it always starts with giving, not some*thing*, but ourselves.

Give yourself first to God. Stop now, and give *yourself*—your breath, your health or sickness, your thoughts, your intents, all of who you are—to him. And your time, that too. Acknowledge that every moment you receive is God's sheer gift. Resolve never to turn it into possession. What you receive as gift you must be willing to impart as gift. Invite God to direct your paths, to lead you in the way everlasting; be open to holy interruption, divine appointment, Spirit ambush (and ask God for the wisdom to know the difference). "Many are the plans in a man's heart," Proverbs says, "but it is the LORD's purpose that prevails" (19:21). Surrender to his purpose with gladness. Vow not to resist or resent it.

Give yourself first to God.

Now the hard thing: give yourself to others. Enter this day with a deep resolve to actually *spend* time, even at times seemingly to squander it, for the sake of purposes beyond your own—indeed, that occasionally subvert your own (remember the good Samaritan?). That person you think is such a bore but who always wants to talk with you: Why not really listen to him? Why not give him, not just your time, but yourself—your attention, your affection, the gift of your curiosity and inquisitiveness?

In God's economy, to redeem time, you might just have to waste some.

Try this for a week, giving the gift of yourself first to God and then to others. Be generous with time.

See if your world isn't larger by this time next week.

SIX

We're Not in Egypt Anymore: *Stopping to Remove the Taskmasters*

Michele has an identical twin, Nicole. Both are beautiful. Early on, I was always stumped by who was who and which was which. They're mirror images: the high, fine cheekbones and the soft, dark eyes, the lilting cadence of speech, the delicate artistry and polished musicianship—these are perfectly duplicated in each.

Around that time, my daughters were captivated by a remake of the movie *Parent Trap*, in which actress Lindsay Lohan single-handedly portrays, with the help of special camera effects, identical twins. The story revolves around the twins' elaborate scheme to pose as each other, a scheme so flawlessly executed that they fool their own parents. Watching it with my daughters, I wondered if Michele and Nicole ever did that, pretended to be the other, just to mess with our heads. Back then, I figured I'd be an easy rube.

But as I got to know the twins better (especially Michele, who goes to church where I'm a pastor; Nicole lives in another town and visits only from time to time), I began to see subtle but distinct differences. Their smiles are not exactly alike. They carry themselves with enough degree of difference that you can distinguish one from the other just by watching their postures, their gestures, their expressions, the way they walk. You can tell by listening to the timbre and texture of their voices. In so many ways they are the same, yet in so many ways each is unique—it's like hearing a single Mozart piece played by two different but equally proficient orchestras.

I've known the twins, especially Michele, for close to a decade now. It would take great cunning indeed for me to mistake one for the other.

The Bible provides two complete renderings of the Ten Commandments, one in Exodus 20, the other in Deuteronomy 5. (*Deuteronomy* literally means "the second law," or "the law once over.") The two renderings are virtually identical. They're conjoined twins, separated by a clean, almost invisible cut. The two versions are so close that the slightest variations between them, like a birthmark on one that's missing on the other, take on large significance. After long association, you can easily spot one from the other.

The two Sabbath commands feature a crucial variation. Exodus says this:

> Remember the Sabbath day by keeping it holy. Six days you shall labor and do all your work, but the seventh day is a Sabbath to the LORD your God. On it you shall not do any work, neither you, nor your son or daughter, nor your manservant or maidservant, nor your animals, nor the alien within your gates. For in six days the LORD made the heavens and the earth, the sea, and all that is in them, but he rested on the seventh day. Therefore the LORD blessed the Sabbath day and made it holy. (vv. 8–11)

Deuteronomy says this:

> Observe the Sabbath day by keeping it holy, as the LORD your God has commanded you. Six days you shall labor and do all your work, but the seventh day is a Sabbath to the LORD your

> God. On it you shall not do any work, neither you, nor your son or daughter, nor your manservant or maidservant, nor your ox, your donkey or any of your animals, nor the alien within your gates, so that your manservant and maidservant may rest, as you do. Remember that you were slaves in Egypt and that the LORD your God brought you out of there with a mighty hand and an outstretched arm. Therefore the LORD your God has commanded you to observe the Sabbath day. (vv. 12–15)

Exodus grounds Sabbath in creation. Deuteronomy grounds it in liberation. Exodus remembers Eden, Deuteronomy Egypt. In Exodus, Sabbath-keeping is about imitating divine example and receiving divine blessing. In Deuteronomy, it is about taking hold of divine deliverance and observing divine command.

Exodus looks up. Deuteronomy looks back. Exodus gives theological rationale for rest, and Deuteronomy historical justification for it. One evokes God's character, the other his redemption. One calls us to holy mimicry—be like God; the other to holy defiance—never be slaves again. One reminds us that we are God's children, the work of his hands, the other that we are no one's chattel, not Pharaoh's, not Nebuchadnezzar's, not Xerxes', not Beelzebub's.

One is invitation. The other is warning.

The Exodus command, with its call to imitation, plays on a hidden irony: we mimic God in order to remember we're not God. In fact, that is a good definition of Sabbath: *imitating God so that we stop trying to be God.* We mirror divine behavior only to freshly discover our human limitations. Sabbath-keeping involves a recognition of our own weakness and smallness, that we are made from dust, that we hold our treasure in clay jars, and that without proper care we break.

This is not true of God. He neither sleeps nor slumbers. He runs no risk of breakdown, burnout, exhaustion, injury. God doesn't need Sabbath or sabbatical. He doesn't pine for vacation. He doesn't require a good night's sleep to clear his head or steady his hand. He doesn't run ragged and run amok, pushing himself beyond his limits, patching himself together between bursts of striving and binges of workaholism. God is not waiting for the weekend.

God is complete without rest.

But not us. For us, rest is indispensable. Indeed, all things not God, all things made by God—goats and oaks, scarab beetles and pine needles, dragon lizards and dragonflies—need rest.

And maybe especially us. Because, unlike goats and beetles and flies and lizards, we try to outwit and outrun our limits. We think we're the exception, the one for whom busyness will translate into fruitfulness. We think, because we've figured ways to build impossibly tall, lithe buildings and dig immensely deep, broad holes, to spy on babies in the womb, to tease out strands of DNA, to send whole computer files from New York to Nairobi in a split second—we think because our industry and ingenuity seem boundless, we can also figure a way around our God-imposed need for stillness. We can't. The need is not conjured away by medication, technology, discipline, cleverness, sheer willfulness. It always comes back to take its due.

So God, knowing both our need and our folly, took the lead. He set the example. Like a parent who coaxes a cranky toddler to lie down for an afternoon nap by lying down beside her, God woos us into rest by resting. "For in six days the LORD made the heavens and the earth, the sea, and all that is in them, but he rested on the seventh day. Therefore the LORD blessed the Sabbath day and made it holy."

God commands that we imitate him in order to discover again that we're not him, and that we need him.

Sabbath is a return to Eden.

That's Exodus.

Deuteronomy, the other twin, gives a different rationale for keeping Sabbath. "Remember that you were slaves in Egypt and that the LORD your God brought you out of there with a mighty hand and an outstretched arm. Therefore the Lord your God has commanded you to observe the Sabbath day."

You were once slaves. There was once a day you were denied any choice in this matter. Rest? Work? There was no option. The choice was made for you, day in, day out. The point was reinforced with bullwhips, in case you missed it or were the least inclined to ignore it. The point was, you worked. Period. Rest was for other people. Rest was for Pharaoh. But Pharaoh couldn't rest if you didn't work—he had such overlarge ambitions, so many things he wanted to accomplish, so many tall, pointy monuments he wanted to be remembered by—somebody had to do it. That somebody, that nobody, was you. And to make sure you did it, and didn't ever, ever, ever slack off, he placed taskmasters over you, to smile sinister smiles and clench their forearms into tight braids of muscle whenever you looked even the tiniest bit as if you might sit down a spell.

That's what life was like before.

God drowned them all. He smote them. He went to extravagant lengths—a full-scale house of horrors, with swarms of gnats, blood-thick waters, hailstones large and hard as fists, and, as a show-stopper, a collapsing wall of sea—just to remove that scourge from among you, to take you away from it and it away from you.

Remember?

Was there something about those days for which you are nostalgic? Is there something back there you miss? Are you lonely tonight, mooning for all those galley masters and pit guards, longing for the sting of their whips and their curses?

Here's the logic of the Sabbath command in Deuteronomy: Don't revive what God has removed. Don't gather and piece back together what God smashed and scattered. Don't place yourself in a yoke that God broke and tossed off with his own hands. Just as we ought not pull asunder what God has joined, so we ought not to join what God has pulled asunder. If you loathed life under the threats and taunts and beatings of taskmasters, why reprise it?

Because that's what the refusal to rest amounts to: living as though the taskmasters still hover and glower, ever ready to thrash us for the smallest sign of slowing down. It is to strive and toil as though we have no choice, as if we'll be punished otherwise.

To refuse Sabbath is in effect to spurn the gift of freedom. It is to resume willingly what we once cried out for God to deliver us from. It is choosing what once we shunned.

Slaves don't rest. Slaves can't rest. Slaves, by definition, have no freedom to rest.

Rest, it turns out, is a condition of liberty.

God calls us to live in the freedom that he won for us with his own outstretched arm.

Sabbath is a refusal to go back to Egypt.

That's Deuteronomy.

There is one very large, very grim obstacle to keeping Sabbath. It is the problem of taskmasters. God drowned the taskmasters, it's true—dragged the whole Egyptian army to the muddy, weedy sea bottom. Only, some survived: they clung to the flotsam of our guilt and worry and ended up marooned in our heads. It's actually worse: we helped them survive. We threw them ropes, pulled them ashore, resuscitated the unconscious ones.

Now, there's a whole noisy, jostling colony of them still with us, and they lapse into old habits the minute we try to rest. They swagger and bark like men in authority—and ought to, since we're inclined to give way. When I try to step back from my day's work, the taskmasters in my head rise up, look at me menacingly, advance toward me.

What do you think you're doing?

Uh, just taking a few minutes to . . . sit down.

You're taking a few minutes to sit down? How quaint. How charming. You're taking a few minutes to sit down, as though there's not a huge, stinking pile of things that you've left undone. You are so weak and pathetic. I'm warning you. There are a thousand things to do. There are a million things to worry about. Get off your lazy, sprawling backside and get busy!

This happened just today—even though I should know better. I lay down for no reason other than to lie down. Within a minute, a taskmaster in my head spotted me, strode over, started his tirade. *When are you going to clean your office? Have you phoned the mechanic yet to have that rattle in your truck motor looked at? What about the situation with that couple at church—when are you going to attend to that? Do you know how many e-mails you haven't responded to? Do you think you can just wile away an hour here on the couch when all this hangs over you? You are so smug, so rude, so slothful. What kind of time-frittering, excuse-mongering sad sack of a sluggard are you anyhow, lolling about as if the work's all done? You should be ashamed of yourself.*

Taskmasters despise rest. They create a culture where rest must be stolen, savored on the sly, and of course then it's not rest: worry over getting caught plunders rest's restfulness. Even if they never lay a hand on you (hard to do, since they're imaginary), they mount a ruthless psychological war, a propaganda campaign at once cunning and artless, that defeats you more than whips.

Maybe you, too, have a taskmaster or three living with you. I am learning how to let them drown.

The power of a lie is its half-truth. Lies that are pure lie—outlandish tall tales, the kind of bizarre claims that tabloid copyists generate by the tonnage (*hotels discovered on Mars, a girl born with devil horns and spike tail in Toledo, a colony of talking geckos in northern Thailand*)—these can be spotted from a great distance, laughed at, discounted, dismissed. Bald-faced lies are just that: bald-faced. They are flat-out obvious. They are a subcategory of slapstick and lampoon.

But most lies aren't like this. Most have a veneer of credibility, a certain intuitive rightness about them. We're inclined to believe them. The lies that do the most damage are never the bald-faced variety. They're the masked-faced variety. They are the lies so intricately webbed with truth that the two, falsehood and truth, are almost impossible to unravel from each other.

I have a good friend who for most of his life believed everything he touched would fail. This was in spite of the fact that he had accumulating evidence—his marriage, his family, his friendships, his business, his faith—that pointed in exactly the opposite direction. His life in the main has been a series of staggering accomplishments. But when he was young, his father told him over and over—and did it with anger, with disgust—that he couldn't do anything right. The way he chopped wood was wrong. The manner in which he took out the garbage was disastrous. His schoolwork was appalling. On and on it went, a swarm of faultfinding.

The thing is, some of this was half true. My friend needed to learn to aim past the wood when he chopped it. He needed to seal the garbage bag more tightly before he carried it out so that rinds and crusts and coffee grounds didn't spill, and to make sure its underside wasn't dripping its thick, sticky ferment of syrup across the kitchen floor. He could have shored up his work in English, paid more attention to the way commas work, the way verbs conjugate and nouns decline.

But the lie that rooted in these half-truths and flourished was this: you can't do *anything* right. And so my friend, believing it, strove and strove—accomplished amazing things with all his striving—and always felt it wasn't enough.

He's much better. He's learned—through a wife who loves him, friends who would take a bullet for him, a church that nourishes him, and a prayer life that has become as important to him as breathing—to spot the lies mixed with the half-truths, learned how to winnow out one from the other.

Here's why I'm telling you this: taskmasters are masters of half-truth. They couch their harangue in just enough reality that the whole thing has the ring of authenticity. It's true, in part, what they say: there *is* no end of things to do. I *am* a touch on the lazy side and disguise this with busyness. There *is* a crowd of people disappointed with me, who find me, by turn, indecisive, despotic, timid, rash, evasive, blunt, foolhardy, wise in my own eyes, foot-dragging, impulsive. I *do* procrastinate overmuch and at the same time make too many snap decisions. Most of my life *is* unfinished. Many of my efforts *are* slapdash and slipshod.

It's true.

So? The lie mixed in here is that, because it's true, I have no right to rest.

And actually, that's true too. I have no right to a lot of things: my health, my home, my family, my salvation. May as well add rest to the list.

But thank God that God could care less about our rights. What God cares about, and deeply, is our needs. And it's this simple: you and I have an inescapable need for rest.

The lie the taskmasters want you to swallow is that you cannot rest until your work's all done, and done better than you're currently doing it. But the truth is, the work's never done, and never done quite right. It's always more than you can finish and less than you had hoped for.

So what? Get this straight: The rest of God—the rest God gladly gives so that we might discover that part of God we're missing—is not a reward for finishing. It's not a bonus for work well done.

It's sheer gift. It is a stop-work order in the midst of work that's never complete, never polished. Sabbath is not the break we're allotted at the tail end of completing all our tasks and chores, the fulfillment of all our obligations. It's the rest we take smack-dab in the middle of them, without apology, without guilt, and for no better reason than God told us we could.

Moses hated taskmasters. He saw their ways with God's people—their loutishness and brutishness, their jackboot tactics—and he got mad. Wrath, wild and blazing and holy, rose up in him. He killed one. He smote him, struck him down hard and fast and very dead.

As a kind of parting indignity, and in a feeble attempt to cover the crime, he buried the man in the sand.

Dust to dust for you.

For that, Moses ended up in exile for forty years, grazing sheep on scrub brush and sere grass. The exile was necessitated by circumstances—he was a fugitive from Egypt—but more than that, it was God's idea. Moses's ploy, it turns out, was ill-conceived. It just made Pharaoh nastier and left the people he was trying to help neither free nor grateful.

It was no way to kill a taskmaster.

In some ways, the whole point of the Exodus was Sabbath. *Let my people go,* became God's rallying cry, *that they might worship me.* At the heart of liberty—of being let go—is worship. But at the heart of worship is rest—a stopping from all work, all worry, all scheming, all fleeing—to stand amazed and thankful before God and *his* work. There can be no real worship without true rest.

Pharaoh, his army, his taskmasters—all stand in the way of both freedom and worship. They are enemies of both, and so enemies of rest. Pharaoh might grant these things—freedom, worship, rest—conditionally or capriciously, in a spree of bigheartedness or a faint spell of repentance. But he's fickle, quick to snatch the gift back, double up the workload.

And he and his crew are not easily removed. There's no lasting fruit from Moses's angry burst of violence. The taskmasters are down one, but their resolve is only multiplied.

Only God can rid us of taskmasters.

Our part is to trust.

To trust.

Ah, how plain and clear that is. How simple, even.

And how hard.

There's a fascinating exchange in John's Gospel between Jesus and the Jews during the Feast of Tabernacles. Jesus, back in Galilee, has a barbed exchange with his own brothers, who try to jeer him into making an appearance at the feast. They want him to pull out all the stops, dazzle the crowd with his wonder-working antics. It's the devil's temptations all over again: *Throw yourself from this temple, turn these stones into bread. . . .* Jesus rebuffs them. But after they leave, he slips into Jerusalem anyhow, stealthy, perhaps disguised, and there mingles with the pressing, searching crowds. There's an atmosphere of heightened anticipation and speculation about his whereabouts, his identity. Who is he? Where is he?

Halfway through the feast, Jesus goes public. He stands up in the temple courts, not to perform miracles, as his brothers advised, but to teach. The crowd is at once captivated and wary, astonished by him, suspicious of him. Is he heaven-sent or hell-bent? Jesus accuses them of trying to kill him, and they answer back, "You are demon-possessed. . . . Who is trying to kill you?" (John 7:20).

Jesus responds to this with an answer that appears to be tossed in from another conversation entirely. Jesus did this often—answered people in a way that sent the discussion at hand careening in a whole new direction. He was master of the non sequitur, genius of the cryptic retort. So it is here:

> Jesus said to them, "I did one miracle, and you are all astonished. Yet because Moses gave you circumcision (though actually it did not come from Moses, but from the patriarchs), *you circumcise a child on the Sabbath. Now if a child can be circumcised on the Sabbath* so that the law of Moses may not be broken, why are you angry with me for healing the whole man on the Sabbath?" (John 7:21–23, emphasis mine)

The miracle Jesus mentions is likely when he healed, either at this feast or at an earlier one, an invalid at the pool in Bethesda. It's recorded in John 5. The man had been lame thirty-eight years, growing hard with despair and raw with self-pity. Jesus sought him out, asked him if he wanted to be healed (to which he got no straight reply), and ordered the man to pick up his mat and walk. The man did and promptly got in trouble with the Jewish establishment for carrying his mat, a breach of Sabbath regulations.

I'll return to this exchange in a later chapter, when we look at the connection between Sabbath and healing. But here I want to tease out a surprising, perhaps quirky, connection between circumcision, healing, and Sabbath. Clearly Jesus's plain meaning is that just as circumcision is a sign of unique belonging to God, of covenant relation, and is therefore most fittingly practiced on the Sabbath, so healing is a sign of God's intimate presence and blessing and thus is best done on the Sabbath. Healing on the Sabbath is just as desirable as circumcision on the Sabbath, since both announce that God is our God and he is for us and not against us.

But I want to look at something other than Jesus's plain meaning. Circumcision, like Sabbath, is also about trust. To be circumcised is to be wounded in a place of intimacy and vulnerability. It is to permit, even invite, an act of violence—a sharp knife, a painful cut, a bloody removal—in that part of a man he otherwise most guards and hides. It is also the part he most intimately joins with a woman. Circumcision is being scarred in a place of deep identity, where a man understands himself to be a man. It is being wounded at the only source where a man can create life. Many parts of a man's anatomy are useful: with his mind he imagines, with his hands he devises, with his feet he deploys. A man can create many things, but only in this one place can he create life. It is here the knife is applied.

The scar, the wound, sets this man apart: it says that here, even here, especially here, he is a marked man. He is one who belongs to God.

That is trust. To allow a hand to wield a knife in this place, to cut such a vulnerable, valuable, intimate part of the man, and for no reason other than that God has chosen this means and this place to mark him—that is supreme trust.

That trust is the hallmark of circumcision comes out in an obscure passage in the book of Joshua. Joshua has led the Israelites across the Jordan and pitched camp on the plains of Jericho. The news that the armies of God are nearby, preparing for attack, has reached the kings of Canaan. The people in the surrounding towns and villages are terrified.

Picture it.

The people of God have gathered in mass assembly. The peaks of their countless tents cut like mountain ranges on the horizon. The smoke from the fires of their many encampments rises like omens against the sky. There is a drone from their workaday conversations, from the clank of metal hitting metal, from the laughter of children playing tag, from the mewling of sheep and the clatter of oxcarts, from a distance it is like the roar of an approaching storm. And so it is. The Amorites and Jebusites and Canaanites and Gibeonites are hardly able to put one foot in front of the other for fear. It's all they think about, all they talk about, all they pray to their gods about. Why plant or harvest, why build or forge, why marry or bear children when this inescapable threat looms close, moves closer?

It's at this moment God gives the strangest command: "At that time the LORD said to Joshua, 'Make flint knives and circumcise the Israelites again.' So Joshua made flint knives and circumcised the Israelites at Gibeath Haaraloth" (Josh. 5:2–3).

It is mostly the young men, the men of fighting age, who undergo circumcision. Israel's brawny warriors are subjected to this deep wounding.

This is just the kind of opportunity Israel's enemies were hoping against hope would come their way: to have the entire Hebrew army laid up, limping and groaning, too weak to pick up kindling wood, let alone brandish a broadsword, too damaged to fling a twig, let alone hurl a spear. Israel carried in its collective memory the story of Jacob's sons, tricksters like their father, who duped the men of Shechem, all fierce warriors, into undergoing circumcision as a kind of bride-price for Jacob's daughter, Dinah. These men accepted the terms and lined up for circumcision. Then, when their wounds were still raw, Jacob's sons went into their city and cut the men down like dry grass (see Gen. 34).

Circumcision makes a man childlike. It makes him defenseless. It incapacitates him, reduces him to cowering helplessness. If Israel's enemies find out this news, that all the soldiers are undone by intimate wounds—and this by the God of Israel's choice—then who needs an army to turn back the threat? A gang of village boys, packing slingshots and sticks, could waltz in and finish the job.

Why didn't God give the order for this a month or two back, on the east side of the Jordan, when the Israelites were not in such an exposed condition and before the fear and hatred of the Canaanites were aroused? If this was only about obedience, that would have been a more logical moment to issue the command. Yet God waited until this moment, when the stakes were precariously high. Why?

Because the whole enterprise was about trust. It was an exercise to teach the Israelites, not just obedience, but dependency: to rely utterly on God and not on themselves. It was the equivalent of what God later did with Gideon, stripping his army to a squad, and then stripping them of weapons, all so that none could boast on the day of victory in their own might or cleverness (see Judg. 6–7).

Circumcision is about trust.

And so is Sabbath. Sabbath is turning over to God all those things—our money, our work, our status, our reputations, our plans, our projects—that we're otherwise tempted to hold tight in our own closed fists, hold on to for dear life. It is allowing God to wound us in an intimate and vulnerable place, to scar us and mark us and make us his own. It is camping circumcised on the plains of Jericho, in striking distance of the enemy. It is letting go, for one day out of seven, all those parts of our identities and abilities in which we are constantly tempted to find our security and discovering afresh that we are his children and that he is our Father and shield and defender.

"And after the whole nation had been circumcised, they remained where they were in camp until they were healed" (Josh. 5:8).

Sabbath is camping out in one place long enough for God to wound us and heal us. It is God's opportunity to demonstrate to us, at the very rim of havoc, on the very outskirts of destruction, his utter trustworthiness. He makes us lie down and prepares a table for us in the presence of our enemies. We learn that here, even here, especially here, his rod and his staff comfort us.

He watches over. You can rest.

G. K. Chesterton told a parable that goes something like this. A young boy was given a choice: he could be gigantic, or he could be minuscule.

He chose to be gigantic.

His head brushed the clouds. He waded the Atlantic like a pond, scooped gray whales into his hand and swished them like tadpoles in the bowl of his palm. He strode in a few bounds from one edge of the continent to the other. He kicked over a range of mountains like an anthill, just because he could and he didn't feel like stepping over it. He plucked a California redwood and whittled its tip for a toothpick. When he got tired, he stretched out across Nebraska and Ohio, flopped one arm into the Dakotas and the other into Canada, and slept in the grass.

It was magnificent. It was spellbinding. It was exhilarating.

For about a day.

And then it was boring. And the gigantic boy, in his boredom, daydreamed about having made the other choice, to be minuscule. His backyard would have become an Amazonian rain forest. His gerbil would hulk larger than a woolly mammoth, and he could ride the back of a butterfly or go spelunking down wormholes. A tub of ice cream would be a winter playground of magic proportions.

Life would have been so much more interesting had he chosen smallness.

You don't need to be big enough to kill taskmasters or tear down enemy walls. You just need to trust in the God big enough to remove them.

Sabbath Liturgy: Relinquishing

The Power of the Powerless is Christopher de Vinck's story about Oliver, Christopher's severely mentally and physically handicapped brother. Oliver never spoke a word, never walked a step, never lifted, not once, a spoon to his own lips. His family tended his stick-limbed body like a baby's—fed and bathed and carried and diapered him—from infancy to his death at age thirty-three. Oliver was mute and helpless, but he was a good teacher. He taught the de Vincks that love is not a fluttering, dizzying emotion, gripping you one day, loosing you the next, but a rock-solid resolve to give yourself, day after day after day, to another.

A few years after Oliver died, Christopher and his son David were planting raspberries together. David saw a beetle scuttling across the earth. Christopher had stopped to talk with a neighbor, and David, five at the time, pointed at the beetle for all to see. There it was, a thing wondrous and strange: amphibian and avian, winged and armored, silently bound to some instinctual duty. Christopher had taught his sons a love of creation. He had taught them to behold God's handiwork with reverence, to handle it with tenderness. He had taught them how to capture, with cup and paper, housebound wasps, and to release them outdoors, their bodies looping away in open air. He had taught them how, before swooping down a park slide, to gently brush the ants off the mirrored metal of its surface into the grass.

So David was captivated by what he saw.

> "Look, Daddy! What's that?" I stopped talking with my neighbor and looked down.
>
> "A beetle," I said.
>
> David was impressed and pleased with the discovery of this fancy, colorful creature.

> My neighbor lifted his foot and stepped on the insect, giving it an extra twist in the dirt.
>
> "That ought to do it," he laughed.
>
> David looked up at me, waiting for an explanation, a reason. I did not wish to embarrass my neighbor, but then David turned, picked up the hose, and continued spraying the raspberries.
>
> That night, just before he turned off the lights in his bedroom, David whispered, "I liked that beetle, Daddy."
>
> "I did too," I whispered back.[1]

I used to think the spiritual life was mostly about finding and using our gifts for God's glory—my utmost for his highest. More and more, I think it is not this, not first, not most. At root, the spiritual life consists in choosing the way of littleness. I become less so that Jesus might become greater. Its essence is *No*—*No* to ourselves, our impulses and cravings, our acts of self-promotion and self-vindication, our use of power for its own sake. It calls us to deny ourselves possessions, rights, conquests that we're tempted to claim just because we can. It is growing, day by day, into the same attitude that Christ had, and by exactly the same means: emptying ourselves, giving ourselves. It is refusing to grasp what we think is owed us and instead embracing what we think is beneath us.

Simply behold, in love and wonder, what you have strength to crush. Exercise power—power you might use otherwise—to serve, bless, protect.

Learn to give and receive.

I have a friend whose son was increasingly unruly and rude to his mother. Whenever the boy stepped over the line, she called in her husband to deal with the child. My friend's default was to use his strength to force reform. He bellowed, threatened, invoked harsh penalties, demanded acts of restitution. It worked. Sort of. His son grudgingly apologized, sullenly conformed, listlessly obeyed. But inside he was growing hard and bitter.

One day the boy breached all boundaries. The mother called for the father, and up the stairs he took his son, to the room where consequences got doled out. He was, my friend, burning with anger, ready to trounce his son. Ready to crush him.

Halfway up the stairs, he was overcome with another idea. *What would love look like now? What shape would servanthood take?* He began to pray, desperately. He reached the landing, walked into the room with his son, sat beside him. The boy wore the look he had perfected for these occasions: a face both taut and slack, a mask of impassiveness to conceal a violent seething. Slowly, quietly, my friend started to tell his son about his own fears. He told him about what had paralyzed him almost lifelong, paths he never walked for fear of losing or failing. He told him about how God was working deep things in him, wrenching and healing things, things he oftentimes wanted to flee or quit except that he didn't want to go back to what was before. He told his son all the things he loved and admired in him, all the ways he believed his son was destined for greatness. He told his son his one repeated prayer for him: that he would surpass him.

The conversation went on a long time. His son's eyes grew big with wonder and his body limber with relief. He began to ask questions. Then my friend asked his son what he wanted to do. He wanted to apologize to his mother and finish the task over which their argument had erupted.

"Good idea," my friend said.

And down the stairs his son went, joyful even in repentance.

Do this: think of a situation where you have been tempted toward, and maybe resorted to, the exercise of sheer power.

What would love look like?

What would servanthood?

Ask God to show you, and then do it.

SEVEN

Losing My Religion: *Stopping Legalism*

Last summer I finally made the journey home, back to southern Ontario. Southern Ontario is not *my* home—I never lived there, and except for two early childhood visits and several recent work-related trips, I've spent little time there. But both of my parents grew up in southern Ontario, in a variety of little towns outside Toronto bearing names—Godrich, London, Waterloo, Breslau, Guelph, Lindsay, Lakefield—that echo cities and towns and villages in the homelands of the German, Dutch, and English immigrants who settled here centuries back, who longed to carry a piece of their own pasts with them and tuck it into the streets and buildings of this new place, hoping it would work its way through, rub its scent into this unfamiliar landscape.

Southern Ontario feels like home to me because so much of my personal history is hidden here. See, that slow brown river is where my dad fished, snagging scowling bass from its reedy shallows. And there's the squat brick house where he grew up, and the upstairs window he crawled out at night to skulk off with his drinking pals. There's the street on which my uncle got hit by a car and dragged thirty feet, and down which my mother ran screaming, announcing, prematurely it turned out, his death. There's the bank where my parents met, two tellers snapping crisp bills or smoothing crumpled ones, shyly glancing at each other across the wickets, seeking opportunities to brush one another's arms and make it seem like clumsiness.

This is home because it's thick with aunts and uncles and cousins I've lived apart from most of my lifetime but whose faces are like looking into mirrors—carnival mirrors that skew you slightly, make your nose thinner or chin longer or forehead wider or ears more crumpled.

It's odd to meet them now, all these years later. We share bloodlines, wide swaths of genetic material, deep pockets of memory. Many of us have eyes the same shade of green, with the same feline glint. Our voices rise and fall with similar pitch and cadence, and this one's laugh—a staccato sharpness with a hint of wheeze—mimics that one's. Our patterns of fretfulness and recklessness and obsessiveness overlap. Many of us like to read the tangled intricacy of maps. We think too much about money and food. We fret about weather, though none of our livelihoods depend on it.

These are people I've been missing my whole life, people who complete me and explain me in many ways. These are intimate strangers. I know them, but not by the usual means. I know them by the whisper of heredity, the thickness of tribal memory, quirks of instinct, rumors of shared wounds. There is, at the roots, a deep-down entanglement. There is a shared cache of private folklore that shapes us.

Sabbath is the stranger you've always known. It's the place of homecoming you've rarely or never visited, but which you've been missing forever. You recognize it the moment you set eyes on it. It's the gift that surprises you, not by its novelty, but by its familiarity. It's the song you never sang but, hearing it now, know inside out, its words and melody, its harmonies, its rhythm, the way the tune quickens just before the chorus bursts. It's been asleep in you all this time, waiting for the right kiss to wake it.

Life is meant to be much different—fuller, richer, deeper, *slower*—from what it is.

You know this. You've always known it.

You've just been missing it your whole life.

But Sabbath is elusive. It is hard to grasp, like the shadow of the wind. Pressures in and around us conspire to muddy our remembrance of it, dry up our keeping of it.

It's like Molvania, that tiny, mountainous, landlocked eastern European country just now emerging from the shadow of Communism. Santo Cilauro, Tom Gleisner, and Rob Sitch have written the definitive travel guide to this old-world nation of shoe cobblers and goat herders. In fact, they've written the *only* travel guide. An old fur-capped man, scruffy-browed and bleary-eyed, grins gap-toothed from the book's cover, holding up a glass of garlic brandy, a traditional Molvanian breakfast drink. Behind him stretches a blighted landscape of stony earth and barren trees. Above him looms a wintry sky.

Everything you ever wanted to know about Molvania—its history and geography, its legends and lore, its ethnic groups and dialects, its quirks and taboos—it's all here. The authors have assiduously researched and compiled, along with maps and charts and photos of historic sites and not-to-be-missed attractions, a wealth of information. Each page has a patchwork of sidebars and insets that are crammed with travel tips and tourist warnings. For instance, on page 85, under the section "Where to Eat?" there's a photo of several shirtless men, their meaty backs lacquered with sweat, bent over plates of food, gobbling like dogs. The caption: "When dining in certain parts of southern Molvania, it is considered rude to ask for cutlery." Or flip back to page 78, under the accommodation section, and find this warning: "Due to erratic water pressure, guests at Vajana's top hotels are advised against using bidets (*frekljsqirts*). As one recent visitor pointed out, 'There's a fine line between personal hygiene and colonic irrigation.'" Every few pages, Philippe, the travel guide's world-weary explorer, weighs in with a bit of hard-won travel wisdom. A sample:

> I was traveling through Svetranj some years ago with a group of friends who suddenly had to leave me. Tired of the usual tourist traps and tacky souvenir shops, I hailed a cab and asked the driver (in my best Molvanian!) to take me somewhere I could get a real sense of the country's heart and soul, somewhere I belonged. Two and a half hours up the road he dropped me off in a vast wilderness that I later recognized as the Great Plain. A few days later, when I collapsed from hunger and hypothermia, I realized it was one of the most authentic travel experiences I ever had. Unforgettable![1]

Quaint. Charming. Exotic.

The whole thing's a spoof.

Molvania—"a land untouched by modern dentistry"—doesn't exist. The authors have gone to elaborate lengths to parody, down to appendices with conversion tables for currency and distances, a serious travel guide. Their mimicry is so note-perfect it takes reading many pages, with increasing double takes, to catch on to the joke.

Everything about Molvania is a hoax.

That's my fear, writing about Sabbath. The thing has proved so elusive, so mirage-like, we're beginning to wonder if it really exists, or whether all books about it are works of clever invention, mythologies disguised as histories, travel guides concocted as parodies of the real thing.

There are two main things that do this, make Sabbath an invented country, a place we read about but never get to.

One is busyness. The other is legalism.

Busyness is more our problem now, and I talked about it earlier. But for a long while, legalism was the hound that chased Sabbath, kept it gaunt and haunted. That certainly was the situation Jesus met up with in Galilee and thereabouts: the towns jostled with sticklers for the rules, men who studied every nuance of Sabbath rigmarole, who watched every move Jesus made, who whipped themselves into every shade of purple over his infractions. They made a kind of sport of it, devising sting operations to see if they could get Jesus to do something outlandish and, in their eyes, illicit on the Sabbath. He typically obliged, knowing full well what they were doing.

The low point, I think, is an event told in all three synoptic Gospels. Jesus heals a man with a shriveled hand, flouting, let's say, Injunction 218, subsection 3c, clause ii, of the *Pharisaical Manual of Rules and Protocols.* The sticklers fly into a rage. Cursing and rending of clothes. Veins bulging from foreheads, cords jutting from necks, fists clenched so tight that fingers flame red and knuckles blanch white. None of this, apparently, forbidden on Sabbath. And then: "The Pharisees went out and began to plot with the Herodians how they might kill Jesus" (Mark 3:6).

Two things are remarkable about this. One, Pharisees and Herodians despised each other. The Pharisees deemed the Herodians toadies of Herod and puppets of Rome, bent on destroying righteousness for the sake of fashionableness. The Herodians saw the Pharisees as reactionary bigots, rednecks and yokels trying to drag the nation back into the dark ages with all their finicky purity laws. To Pharisees, Herodians were soft as rot. To Herodians, Pharisees were brittle as blown glass. Each group represented to the other everything wrong with Israel—which makes them, of course, reminiscent of certain groups alive and well today.

Yet they unite over a common enemy: Jesus. Jesus has so affronted their very different scales of values that they will link arms to eliminate him.

The second remarkable thing is that they plot murder on the Sabbath. As they see it, healing on the Sabbath is forbidden, but plotting murder is perfectly acceptable. This is legalism at its most flagrant. Legalism is the reduction of life to mere technicalities. It substitutes code for conscience, ritual for worship, rectitude for holiness, morality for purity. The most bizarre lines of reasoning appear completely natural to a legalist: you must never heal on the Sabbath, but you can plot the death of those who do.

For the longest while I felt a smug pleasure in sitting in judgment of these legalists. And then I realized I was one of them. At the very least, I was keeping score of their keeping score. But that was, indeed, the very least. It went much deeper than that. As I started to keep Sabbath, I noticed the exact same tendencies they exhibited taking root in me. I developed some rules, good rules, I thought, but rules all the same. At first I exhorted myself to keep the rules. Then I castigated myself for not keeping the rules. Then I prided myself for keeping them, if not perfectly, then at least better than other people did. Then I started to find fault with those other people, people who didn't have the same rules I had or who didn't keep the rules as consistently as I did. Then I found myself getting angry with those people when they dared to feel tired or stressed. *Well, if you had kept the Sabbath holy—as I do—you wouldn't feel that way, now, would you?*

It's not too far from here to plotting murder.

The attraction of legalism is that, despite all its complexity, it's mindless. It requires little or no personal engagement. It's sheer mechanics, simple arithmetic, no more difficult than cranking a hoist or measuring a length of board. You just follow orders. You match the parts to the diagram and apply pressure. It need draw nothing from your heart, your mind, your strength, your soul. It's like paint-by-numbers: it requires no artistry, no imagination, no discipline, just dumb, methodical obedience.

And the attraction of legalism is its inherent rewards. Legalism feels good, in a perverse sort of way. It strokes our egos, fills us with the pleasure of achievement, knowing we spelled all the words correctly, and in such a nice, tidy script to boot. And it's even better if we accomplish this where others have failed. It's like winning a race: it wouldn't mean half as much—indeed, it wouldn't mean anything—if our triumph didn't imply others' losses. The secret impetus behind legalism is its competitiveness. The point is not just to win: *it's to beat everyone else.* Read "beat" in that last line however you wish.

But is Sabbath-keeping inherently this way, rulebound and rival-mongering? It certainly seems so, since every time we've paid it any mind, we've ended up in a tangle of injunctions and imperatives and comparisons.

But then there's Jesus.

Jesus broke virtually all the Pharisees' Sabbath rules. He blew them over like card houses, dismissed them as man-made claptrap. Jesus provoked his opponents as much by his aloofness as by his defiance: he just didn't seem to care that they had worked so hard on their code books, on the intricacies of policy and etiquette, on spelling out in infinite and infinitesimal fine print dos and don'ts by the armloads. One minute, Jesus seemed to break their rules as an impish prank, a way of getting their goat, and the next as a holy crusade, a full assault on their arrogant presumption. Yet he couldn't have cared less about winning or losing; some other standard of conduct motivated him.

It makes you wonder: Does God have any rules about Sabbath? Or did we make them all up ourselves?

It turns out, God gave only broad and general prescriptions for the Sabbath—cease work, mainly—and here and there an oblique clue. The only incident where a real and actual rule is broken is in Numbers 15, and we learn about the rule in the breach, through the breaking of it. A man is caught gathering brushwood on the Sabbath. Those who catch him haul him in to see Moses and Aaron—implying that this is a serious matter, since Moses long ago established that he would handle only the weightiest rulings (see Exod. 18). Moses asks God what is to be done, and God invokes the death penalty (this is likely the proof text Jesus's opponents were thinking of when they sought to stone him).

But such living by its very nature is deadly. Anxiety and stress are our number one killers. I heard recently a story about Meyer Friedman, the psychologist who devised the Type A/ Type B personality profiles—

where Type B is placid and limber, taking life as it comes, and Type A is two-fisted and bristling, taking life by the horns. Friedman's initial insight that led to his personality theory came after a discussion with a chair upholsterer. The upholsterer said that most of his business came from replacing the upholstery on the chairs in cardiologists' offices, the chairs wore first, and quickly, on the front edge. Apparently, heart patients are so impatient that, even while listening to their doctor's life-threatening diagnosis or lifesaving prescription, they sit taut and restless, poised to flee, chafing at the delay.[2] At the edge of their seats. The very reason their hearts are sick is written in that threadbare upholstery.

It's killing us, our worry, our hurry, our need to gather one more armload of brushwood, our haste to get out of the heart doctor's office and back to the fast food and the fast lane. We take our rat poison to thin our blood clots and scurry back to the rat race to clot our blood some more. The death verdict is inscribed in this way of life.

Not long ago, I was trimming my lawn in a terrible hurry. I had a stack of chores to do, and daylight was fading. I was in too much of a hurry to hunt down my safety glasses that day. I was almost running with the weed trimmer, muttering near-expletives every time its aging motor stalled. I was praying—I'm not kidding—that the cutting cord wouldn't run out before I finished. At the edge of the front garden, I held the head of the weed trimmer close to the ground to scalp the lawn, to scrape it down to bare earth. The whirring cords plucked an embedded stone and, like David with his slingshot, flung it hard into my left eye. I fell, clutching my face, yelping. When I got up, I could barely see. My injured eye felt like the chunk of rock had slivered into it. I pried my eye open to make sure I still had sight. The sun's brightness stung my retina. My vision was waterlogged. The world looked as the sea does when I'm diving and my mask fills up. I had to shut the hurt eye. My good eye, in sympathy, shut too.

I staggered into the house, groped my way into the bathroom, scooped cold water onto my face. I rummaged through the medicine cabinet, tipping and scattering bottles and vials, looking for an eye patch. None. I sacked my wife's makeup tray and found cotton pads, the kind she uses to swab off cosmetics.

And what did I do with these? I stuck three of them, with Scotch tape, to my injured eye, then went out and finished the trimming.

I just couldn't stop. When would the work get done if not now?

Later, reflecting on my drivenness, I felt a deep and shameful kinship with that nameless man in Numbers, picking up sticks, packing one more fistful of twigs under his arm. Not able to stop.

But apart from that one story in the Bible, it's silent on specific rules. This silence is curious. Elsewhere, in Leviticus, Exodus, Numbers, and Deuteronomy, God prescribes explicit and detailed instruction regarding sexual conduct, priestly garments, dietary concerns, the removal of mildew, the kinds of polyester forbidden. But on Sabbath, almost nothing, only the repetition of general guidelines: rest, cease from work, celebrate, remember, observe, deny yourself, delight yourself.

I think God must be protecting us here from our temptation to clutter simple things. Where in other matters—diet, dress, sex, hygiene—God felt the need to spell things out in tedious and meddlesome detail, here he's taciturn, vague, dropping random clues, giving only broad hints.

Sabbath-keeping is more art than science. It is more poetry than arithmetic. It is something we get a knack for more than memorize procedures about. It is like painting: Done by numbers, it comes off stiff and blotchy. But done with discipline and imagination and passion, it both captures and enhances life.

Isaiah sets up an odd tension that reinforces that more-art-than-science nature of Sabbath-keeping:

> "If you keep your feet from breaking the Sabbath
> and from doing as you please on my holy day,

if you call the Sabbath a delight
and the LORD's holy day honorable,
and if you honor it by not going your own way
and not doing as you please or speaking idle words,
then you will find your joy in the LORD,
and I will cause you to ride on the heights of the land
and to feast on the inheritance of your father Jacob."
The mouth of the LORD has spoken. (Isaiah 58:13–14)

If you do not go your own way, you will find your joy. We keep Sabbath by both a refusal and a pursuit: we refuse to go our own way, and yet we pursue our own joy. Legalism wants to name, in every jot and tittle, both that refusal and that pursuit. It seeks to pinpoint the precise nature of what we're to shun and what we're to run after.

But God leaves such things unspoken.

Yet clearly, doing as we please, going our own way, is not the same thing as finding our joy. These, in fact, are opposites.

Most of us know this already.

We know that when we do as we please and go our own way, we often as not court misery. We demand our inheritance, squander it, and end up in a pigpen, hungry and spent. This is one of the largest ironies and mysteries of being human: we insist, with pride and stubbornness, on getting our own way, even when that way plunders us wholesale. Paul describes it this way: "For I have the desire to do what is good, but I cannot carry it out. For what I do is not the good I want to do; no, the evil I do not want to do—this I keep on doing. . . . For in my inner being I delight in God's law; but I see another law at work in the members of my body, waging war . . ." (Rom. 7:18–19, 22–23).

Sabbath rest is negotiated in that space between not getting or going our own way and finding our true joy.

I discovered that in my postgraduate year of university. I began then to visit my wife's ailing grandma Christie. I knew Grandma

Christie—Jean Christie—only when she was old, her hair downy fine and bluish white, her skin creased and fragile like crepe paper. I had never known the hearty, wise, fierce, shrewd, tender woman my wife and her cousins described. I knew Jean only in her decline.

The Alzheimer's that would finally ruin her mind was already eroding its edges, making it hard for her to remember simple facts, pull up common words. She was sweet—not cloyingly so but sweet like a fall apple, and with just enough of the Scottish Calvinist crispness of her upbringing still in her to know the sweetness wasn't to be presumed upon. She was the family matriarch, indulged and revered by her eight children and many grandchildren, and increasingly her great-grandchildren.

So it was hard for many of them to watch her fail. Her memory got rapidly worse. She spun off into long, garbled soliloquies, involving people and places she must have known years before, in the old country. They were just strangers and rumors to everyone else. Her mind was a tottering house haunted by childhood ghosts. She talked almost constantly, a slurry of broken words and jumbled thoughts. She puffed up like raised dough from some new medication and then wizened up like a raisin from loss of appetite.

So the family did the hard thing and placed her in a care facility—just to get some meat on her bones, and then she'd move back. In the meantime Cheryl and I, newly married, moved into Grandma Christie's town house, to tend it in her absence.

She never came back. She deteriorated. Her memory darkened or went snowy blank—however these things happen—and she fell mostly silent. She barely ate. Her skin sank into her bones.

It was around then I had a deep conviction that I was to visit her, weekly. I can't remember who else visited her regularly. I had only the conviction that I was to do so. But I didn't want to go. I had been a few times before, with Cheryl, and it scared me: the ward's biting smell of urine that no amount of scouring with bleach could expunge, the musty old man with the blighted eye, cursing Germans, the woman tied to her wheelchair, haggard and brambly haired, who clutched a life-size baby doll and made a shrill and spooky sound like an infant crying. The nurses were gruff and imperious, tired of what was, in effect, a room full of large and unkempt toddlers who needed feeding, changing, bathing, chasing down, cleaning up after, breaking up squabbles among.

This is where Jean was, bedridden.

I had to force myself to go at first. If I hadn't the deep conviction, the sense that God was asking me to do this, I wouldn't have done it for anything. Even then, I made excuses, begged off the first day I intended to go on some minor distraction. But finally I tightened my resolve, and I went. After that, I went almost every week.

And liked it. Loved it, even. It got so it was one of the highlights of my week (there was also playing hockey late Sunday nights, and every Friday morning treating myself, upon a 7:30 arrival on campus, to a large coffee and a gooey cinnamon bun warm from the oven in the student cafeteria). But seeing Jean was one of the things I looked forward to most. It was good to be able to put my books aside, step out into fresh air, drive to the hospital, and find Jean where I'd last seen her, in her bed by the window. She was completely silent now, only a thin Mona Lisa smile on her face and a faraway gaze in her pale blue eyes. I discovered what people so often do in situations like this: that I began going for her sake, but kept going for my own. I went, in sheer obedience, to be a blessing—and ended up receiving one. I would return from my time with her feeling as though I had entertained angels.

Jean died the year Cheryl and I moved away. The family asked me to do the funeral, which was an honor deeper than any of them knew. There were many eulogies from her children and grandchildren. I was surprised by much of what they said. They talked about a woman I didn't know, never had the pleasure of meeting—a woman young, spry, feisty, frugal with money, spendthrift in everything else.

I knew only a woman frail and quiet, a woman, I think, content just to wait. She was a woman who heard things, things no one else had ears to hear. She was a woman whose eyes shone and grew clear when you spoke her name but otherwise had in them the mist of a thousand miles. She was a woman whose lips crimped in the way people's do when they know a good secret but aren't letting on.

Visiting her that first time, I had to fight against doing as I pleased. I had to resist going my own way. If I'd done that, gone there, I'd never have visited Jean. But I obeyed what I believed God told me to do.

And there, in the most unlikely place, I found my joy.

That's a long story to make a brief point: that Sabbath-keeping is grounded in a stark refusal we make to ourselves ("It is a sabbath of rest," Leviticus 16:31 says, "and you must deny yourselves"). We stand ourselves down. We resist that which six days of coming and going, pushing and pulling, dodging and weaving, fighting and defending have bred into us. What we deny ourselves is all our well-trained impulses to get and to spend and to make and to master. This day, we go in a direction we're unaccustomed to, unfamiliar with, that the other six days have made to seem unnatural to us. We do this, this traveling in the opposite direction, maybe for no higher reason at first than that God told us to do it.

But joy is found here. The time you spend playing soccer with your children, or antique-shopping with your spouse, that you otherwise might have spent writing memos for Monday morning or scrubbing walls for your in-laws' visit next week—that time turns out to be a blessing as much for you, maybe more, than for them.

The law of Sabbath is not legalistic. It is a command given to save us from ourselves. If anything, the Sabbath command breaks us out of the prison of our own selfishness: it undoes our legalistic bent to go our own way.

One evening I was preparing for a trip that I had to take the following morning. Cheryl was out, and it was my job to get the girls in bed. I was grumpy about that. I wanted to rush them through their bedtime routines. I was legalistically bound to my own timetable. That's what I wanted: to go my own way, please myself.

"Read us a story, Dad."

I had no intention of reading them a story. I was too busy. I had too many things to do. I got them a snack and told them to brush up, get in bed, go to sleep.

"Please, Dad."

I stopped. I slowed.

I went in the other direction.

"You girls want a story?"

"Yes!"

"Which one?"

"You choose!"

So I went to their room and looked at the books. I have my favorites: Max Lucado's *Just in Case You Ever Wonder*, Phoebe Gilman's *Something from Nothing*, Robert Munsch's *Love You Forever*, Margery Williams's *The Velveteen Rabbit*, a few others. The girls always expect me to pick one of these when they give me the choice.

But something else caught my eye: Dr. Seuss's *Mr. Brown Can MOO! Can You?*, a primer for very young children, children who are a long way off from reading on their own, who are just beginning to explore the world of sounds. My girls outgrew this book years back.

I picked it and hid it behind my back—our routine when I choose the book, so they have to guess which one I've got. They went through the usual suspects. No, no, no, no. I started laughing, couldn't stop. I pulled the book out from behind my back, and they laughed too.

"Sit up straight, children. We're going to read." So, with Sarah on my left and Nicola on my right, we began: "Oh, the wonderful things Mr. Brown can do! He can go like a cow. He can go MOO

MOO. Mr. Brown can do it. How about you?"[3] And then, laughing hard enough to cry, we all let out bullhorn rumbles of long, cacophonous moos.

On it went: squeaking like shoes, buzzing like bees, sizzling like sausage, whispering like the flap of butterfly wings. We laughed the whole way through.

They went to bed happy, and I got on with my work, happy myself, and productive. I finished in plenty of time.

The next morning I was downstairs reading my Bible when the girls awoke. I heard their footfalls on the floor above me. I heard them go into the kitchen and their mother greet them, ask what they wanted for breakfast.

And then I heard something that filled me with wonder. It filled me with joy. My two girls, Sarah, Nicola, sat at the table and mooed like Mr. Brown, then fell into a fit of giggles.

And to think I almost went my own way and missed that.

Sabbath Liturgy:
Finding Your Joy

If I live to decrepit old age, tottering in body and wandering in the head, I still think I won't have deciphered an everyday mystery: how it is we seldom choose what's best. How, given an entire orchard, we'll choose the one fruit forbidden. How, invited into intimacy, we'll settle for suspicion, and encouraged to speak truth in love, we'll instead resort to gossip. How, told not to be anxious about anything but to pray about everything, we'll be anxious anyhow, and more or less prayerless.

Some of the most gifted people I've met are also some of the most broken. Their giftedness has not led them to a place of serenity and thankfulness. It's not led them to what's best. In some cases, it's led to barrenness: fretting, blaming, self-pity, envy, accusation. I know. I fight this in myself daily. My giftedness—modest as it is—has fed my insecurity more times than it has helped me vanquish it. I rarely rejoice in the times I think I have spoken or written well. It produces in me something more akin to panic: *Can I do it again? Did I really do it then? If I'm doing well, why don't more people say so? What's wrong with them? What's wrong with me?*

In quietness and rest is your salvation, God says. But we want to flee and amass horses, chariots, accolades, pats on the back—just about anything to bolster our sense of security and worthiness. But none of those things can. All they do is send us scurrying in the opposite direction. They just widen the hole we want them to fill. Like gluttony, insecurity's appetite increases with every bite.

What a surprising cure God provides: to choose our own joy. God invites that, but with a caution: don't mistake your joy for your druthers. This is not about getting your own way. This is not about indulging your own appetites or satisfying your own sense of justice. This is not about getting what you think is owed you.

This is about finding what is best.

In Luke's story of Mary and Martha, Martha is all in a flap over what she sees as Mary's laziness. Mary sits attentive at Jesus's feet, while Martha wrestles the crockery, thickens the sauce, bastes the lamb chops, sets the table. Mary is oblivious, dreamy and serene, even though Martha is sending up smoke signals thick and menacing. She places the tableware with an emphatic *clunk*. She raps the ladle on the pot's edge hard as a blacksmith nailing horseshoes. She sighs with a hiss like fire brazing water.

Still Mary doesn't notice.

So the lid finally boils over. Martha vents her frustration on both Jesus and Mary: "Lord, don't you care that my sister has left me to do the work by myself? Tell her to help me!" (Luke 10:40).

Jesus gently chides Martha, gently commends Mary. But it's his praise of Mary that should give us pause: "Mary has chosen what is better" (v. 42).

Mary's choice is only *better.*

What would be *best*?

My guess: Martha's industry joined to Mary's attentiveness. Martha's briskness and energy and diligence stemming from Mary's quietness and restfulness and vigilance. The best is to have Martha's hands and Mary's heart.

Here's today's Sabbath Liturgy: sit with Jesus until you hear from him what he would have you do—sit some more, visit the aging, teach Sunday school, or clean your desk. Or, maybe, cook the lunch. And then put your hand to the task, Martha-like, and do it with all your heart, Mary-like.

That's best.

In that, you'll find your joy.

THE GOLDEN RULE: *Stopping to Find a Center*

I learned a valuable life lesson when I was, oh, seven. My mother stepped out to go somewhere—the store for milk, or a friend's house for coffee, or maybe for a walk to clear her head. I don't remember. She asked my nine-year-old brother and me to look after things. (This was the era when parents did such things, and rather often—left young children home alone or loosed them to wander city blocks, neighborhood parks, adjacent woods unattended—and did it without fear of stalking child abductors waiting to waylay them or snooping neighbors, ready to call in the social workers.) Mother told us, specifically, unambiguously, *not to touch* the chocolate cake she had just made. She couldn't have been more clear about that.

I heard her.

I also heard what she didn't say: she never said we couldn't help ourselves to the chocolate cake's chocolate icing. She *clearly* never said that. Cake, after all—even a child knows this—is a substance made from flour, sugar, eggs, a few other powdery things, all mixed and baked. Cake, strictly speaking, is not icing. Icing is what you put on cake once it cools. Cake is cake with or without it.

And that icing was a revelation—a frosting of fudgy goop, lustrous and thick, teased by mother's deft spatula work into a labyrinth of crevices and ridges.

So, clearly hearing what Mother said and what she didn't say, I helped myself to the icing. I began by scooping with one finger the daubs of icing spattered around the foil base the cake sat on. This was, when you think about it, a favor I was doing my mother. I was cleaning up after her. But the taste of that confection in my mouth whet my appetite. I proceeded to scoop, with two fingers, the rim of frosting that drooped down the cake's sides and bulged thick at its base. My fingers left there a double-grooved gouge. I was just getting started. I next skimmed off, with the spatula, what I would have reasonably argued was excess frosting on the top, and then along the sides. Then, to cover my deed, I tried with the same spatula to tease the icing back into that whipped texture at which my mother was such a skilled hand. But I didn't have the knack. Besides, the frosting by this time was crusting slightly, losing its pliancy. When I'd finished, the icing was pitted and chopped, as if a dog had mauled it.

I got found out, of course. I don't remember what consequences I was made to suffer. I do remember, though, my mother scolding me to the effect: "Don't touch the cake means *don't touch the cake*—any of it, all of it, the whole thing."

I gravitate toward minimalism when it comes to obedience. My default is, *What's the least I'm required to do and the most I can get away with?* Show me a command, and I'll show you wondrous interpretive tricks to sidestep its sharper edges and dance around its outer bounds. I will perform astonishing contortionist and escapist techniques worthy of the Ringling Brothers—squirming through tiny loopholes, bending around unmovable objects, wriggling out of padlocked straitjackets, slipping snakelike from ironclad cargo trunks. I will show you how to thread a camel through a needle's eye or swallow one whole and strain out a gnat.

The problem, though, is that minimalist obedience is really no obedience at all. It is a bony, gristly thing, lacking suppleness and muscle, bereft of beauty. A patron saint of minimalism is Jonah, quarreling and sulking outside Nineveh, doing what he's told but refusing to like it. It's the older brother of the prodigal, accusing and complaining outside the father's house, never disobedient but bitter in obeying. These are people who, in a strict ledger book of obedience, have met all basic requirements.

But their hearts are stones.

I was a flagrant Sabbath-breaker. I didn't pay the least bit of heed to the rest of God for almost twenty years of Christian faith. I wish I could say that what finally caught my attention was a conviction of the Spirit brought on by a careful exegesis of biblical texts, a deep meditation on rabbinical writings, a still, small voice wooing me in deeper. But that would be lying. The conviction, the study, the meditation, the voice—they came, but they came late, as a consequence of my interest in rest and Sabbath. What actually finally caught my attention was that I wasn't doing well. Plain and simple, I was worn out. I knew that if I didn't recover the art of rest—if I failed to find the rest of God—I would watch all my works and all my days turn to blight. I became, as I shared earlier, a Sabbath-keeper the hard way.

But a funny tendency emerges in those of us who desire Sabbath-keeping: first, we tend to overdo it, piling rule upon rule. And then, weary with that, we push toward minimalism, discovering loopholes, inventing exemptions, rigging shortcuts. We turn first to legalism and then to excuse making. We spin elaborate definitions, then absolve ourselves on minor technicalities. So we say we won't shop. Not at all. And then one Sunday afternoon we see that if the kids are to have breakfast Monday morning, we need milk. We explain to ourselves that this falls under the category of a bull falling into a well on the Sabbath. *Of course you pull it out.* Well, likewise, if the kids don't eat breakfast or eat their cereal dry and without the recommended daily requirements of calcium and vitamin D, then they will have insufficient strength that day—not to mention bad attitudes—and will struggle to concentrate, and then they'll fall behind in their schoolwork, and then they'll fail third grade, and then their self-esteem will plummet, and then they'll turn to a life of crime and waste and dissipation to fill the void—and all this because I was too hidebound to go out and buy a jug of milk. And so I go and buy the milk, and while I'm at it, I figure I may as well do the grocery shopping I planned to do on Monday, since it's a waste of precious petroleum reserves to make two trips in a week to the grocery store when I could easily combine them into a single trip. And—this clinches it—shopping now will free up more time to rest later on.

And on and on the switchback logic goes.

It tires me just thinking about it. Sabbath-keeping was always meant to be robust, not this picking of bones.

There is a word you may not know or, if you do, likely never use: *synecdoche.* Synecdoche (pronounced si-neck-dah-key with the emphasis on the *neck* sound) is a technical literary term. It means when a single part of some large, complex system stands for the whole: when "the crown" stands for the entire tradition and history of royalty, or "the flag" for all the complex layers of patriotism, or "the cloth" for the practice and personnel of ordained ministry, or "Nam" for the whole experience, the blood and madness, of the Vietnam War. When a word or image functions in this way, it's synecdochic.

I tell you that to tell you this: the Ten Commandments are synecdochic. Each command means more than itself. Each is a tiny part that stands for a vast whole. So when we are commanded, for instance, not to steal, the command stretches beyond bare-bones decree. It means more than simply to restrain your hand from brigandage or thievery. It implies a whole way of life: the practice of contentment, the disciplining of appetites, the deepening of trustworthiness, the enlargement of generosity. The refusal to steal, no more, no less, is a rickety and stingy obedience. It's hardly life to the full. It's obedience to the letter of the law, but not its spirit. A mere abstainer can still be a thief at heart: hoarding, envying, coveting, a skinflint to the last breath. Scrooge-like.

But hear the command synecdochically, and it becomes an invitation to bountiful living—to receive but never take, to give and expect nothing in return, to celebrate the muchness of creation and relationship. It is an invitation to be as Scrooge after his three night visits, spendthrift and giddy, aprowl for opportunities to lavish gifts on friends, strangers, paupers, passersby. It is to be as Zacchaeus after Jesus came to his home, where an outburst of generosity instantly supplants a lifetime of greed. This is the essence, this life of abundance, of the command "Thou shalt not steal."[1]

The commandments call us, not to bare minimalism, not to rigid observance or to tedious ledger toting, but to an exuberant overcompensation—to Zacchaeus-like extravagance. Each command is a doorway into a vast world that is ancient and new all at once.

This is true about the Sabbath command. Interestingly, it is only one of two of the Ten Commandments phrased in a positive manner. Except for this command and the one to honor our parents, all the rest are cast in the "Thou shalt not" form. They are written prohibitively. They take the shape of warnings and shunnings. But the Sabbath command is written in strong imperatives: *remember, observe, keep, stop*. It does get around to prohibition—thou shalt do no work—but this is couched first in the insistence that we do something, something good and hearty and life-giving.

A legalistic disposition, on the one hand, makes the commandment gloomy. It corrals us into a tight corner and forces us to sit, stock-still and long-faced, thinking solemn Sabbath thoughts (*remember, observe, keep, stop*). A minimalist mind-set, on the other hand, gets us looking for shortcuts, ways the commandment can be shaved here, bent there, sloughed off outright over here.

A synecdochic imagination does something utterly new. It invites us into a place that is larger than all the other days—a place so large, in fact, it contains all the other days and at the same time transcends them. It is a day as different from those other days as an ocean is from a lagoon. Each contains the other but transcends it. In doing so it becomes something altogether different.

Sabbath is that day in which all other days have no claim. Monday morning, Wednesday afternoon, Friday evening—none can make demands on Sabbath. Sabbath exists free of their concerns and their obligations. Sabbath owes them no allegiance. It releases us from paying them tribute. For this one day, we can hold aloof from all the other days.

J. R. R. Tolkien gives one of the most entrancing descriptions of the true nature of Sabbath. In book 1 of The Lord of the Rings trilogy, he describes a time of rest and healing in the house of Elrond in Rivendell. The hobbits, along with Strider, their guide, have made a dangerous, almost fatal journey to this place. They will soon have to make an even more dangerous, almost certainly fatal journey away from this place. But in the meantime, this:

> For awhile the hobbits continued to talk and think of the past journey and of the perils that lay ahead; but such was the virtue of the land of Rivendell that soon all fear and anxiety was lifted from their minds. The future, good or ill, was not forgotten, but ceased to have power over the present. Health and hope grew strong in them, and they were content with each day as it came, taking pleasure in every meal, and in every word and song.[2]

The future, good or ill, was not forgotten, but ceased to have power over the present. That's Sabbath.

Lauren Winner, in her book *Mudhouse Sabbath*, remarks on the different wording that Exodus and Deuteronomy use in prescribing the fourth commandment. Exodus calls us to *remember* the Sabbath, Deuteronomy to *observe* it. Why this variation? Winner, a convert first to Judaism and then to Christianity, cites a rabbinical insight: the three days that follow Sabbath are to be spent in reflection upon—*remembering*—the one just past, and the three days leading up to Sabbath are to be spent in preparation for—*observing*—the one approaching.[3] In other words, Sabbath makes claims on all the other days, they make none on it.

To approach Sabbath with synecdochic imagination, and to free Sabbath-keeping from the demands of the other days of the week, one thing is indispensable: *to cease from that which is necessary.* This is Sabbath's golden rule, the one rule to which all other rules distill. *Stop doing what you ought to do.* There are six days to do what you ought. Six days to be caught in the web of economic and political and social necessity.

And then one day to take wing.

Sabbath is that one day. It is a reprieve from what you ought to do, even though the list of oughts is infinitely long and never done. Oughts are tyrants, noisy and surly, chronically dissatisfied. Sabbath is the day you trade places with them: they go in the salt mine, and you go out dancing. It's the one day when the only thing you must do is to not do the things you must. You are given permission—issued a command, to be blunt—to turn your back on all those oughts. You get to willfully ignore the many niggling things your existence genuinely depends on—and is often hobbled beneath—so that you can turn to whatever you've put off and pushed away for lack of time, lack of room, lack of breath. You get to shuck the *have-tos* and lay hold of the *get-tos.*

So can I or can I not chop wood on Sabbath? Well, is it *necessary*? Is it something I *must do*, that I feel under obligation to do? Then no, I won't. It smells like an ought.

But I often chop wood for the sheer exhilaration of it. It makes me feel alive. It puts me in touch with earth and sky, savoring the saltiness of my sweat, the good ache in muscles seldom used, the folksy music of dry alder cracking under the swing of my maul. The same goes with cutting grass. A rhythm and luxury are there that, for me, are the exact opposite of work. The work I do most every other day—that I *must* do—involves reading, writing, preaching, teaching, counseling, attending meetings. I sit around a lot, advising actions, plotting courses, preparing speeches. I make numerous phone calls and always have a few dozen e-mails in the bottleneck. I talk and talk and talk, I write and write and write. To cut the grass, most times at least, pours something back into me that all that other work siphons off. It feels like playing hooky. It feels like getting a barely legal tax break. It feels like a night on the town.

I even shop sometimes. I try to avoid the getting-the-milk-for-the-kids'-breakfast kind of shopping (though I'm not perfectly consistent here and would like to excuse myself by declaring, loud and proud, that I'm no legalist: the truth is, I'm just inconsistent). But if Cheryl and I and our children are driving home on a summer evening from a river where we've spent the afternoon swimming and then falling asleep warming ourselves on the sunbaked rocks, and we pass a roadside fruit stand and I say, "Oh, look at those plums!" or if we are returning on a wintry twilight from a snowy hill where we've just spent an hour or two swooping and tumbling earthward in inner tubes and magic carpets, and we drive by a country quilt shop and Cheryl says, "Oh, look at those pillowcases!"—well, in either case, neither of us turns all stern and scowly and starts haranguing the other about a lack of piety.

We stop, we shop, we buy.

And that touches on Sabbath's second golden rule, or the other half of the first golden rule: *to embrace that which gives life.* The first golden rule, or the first half of it, is *to cease from that which is necessary.* But to be synecdochic in our approach, we need this other part. We need to know, not just what to avoid, but what to pursue.

What defines the shape and nature of that pursuit? Simple: life, and life abundant. When Jesus broke man-made Sabbath regulations, he always went in this direction: he healed, he fed, he claimed the right to rescue creatures fallen into wells or to lead to wells creatures falling down with thirst. Jesus pursued those things that give life. Whatever had been stolen by sickness, by the devil, by sheer accident and mishap—these things he sought to take back and give back. He honored our created limits and restored our created greatness. He did this always and told us to do likewise, but he especially favored the Sabbath for such activity. What better day than Sabbath to trounce Beelzebub, to trump death, to reverse sickness, to repair injury, to pamper ourselves?

Students of the Sabbath have long noted that the command implicitly forbids creating. God created for six days, but on the seventh he rested. So too us: we can create like mad all the other six days of the week—forge widgets, write sermons, send memos, cook muffins, groom poodles, nail house frames, mix concrete, solve riddles. But the seventh day is when we step back and simply enjoy creation. We stop trying to make anything and instead let the things we've made bless and serve us.

Stop creating is the sum of it. This is clear enough, but I find it puzzling, and more than a little susceptible to all the finicky rule-making I, at least, am prone to get into. Is chopping wood creating? What if I write a letter to my aunt—is this different from all the other writing I do, and if so, how? Can I or can I not bake macaroons with my daughters?

But even to ask such things is to lack synecdochic imagination. What is also implicit in the Sabbath command is our need for restoration. God ceased from creating, not because he needed rest or restoration, but because we do and God wanted to set the precedent, to lead by example.

We need to be re-created after all our creating. Creating taps us out. It doesn't have this effect on God, of course. But we're not God. Creating, as invigorating as it can be at times, can also be boring, blistering, depleting. Our resources are limited. Our creativity is easily spent. Creating wears us threadbare. Sabbath is not for more creating. It is for re-creating.

Again, what category does wood chopping, antique shopping, grass cutting, cookie baking, or letter writing fit with you? Is it something you create, or something that re-creates you? Choose the re-creative thing on Sabbath.

Cease from what is necessary. Embrace that which gives life. Those two things, taken together, make up Sabbath's golden rule. They are, to begin with, deep-rooted in Scripture. But they are also simple and versatile, two qualities not to be underrated. Jesus, after all, and after him Peter and Paul, and after them the early church, worked out of an understanding of Sabbath that had these qualities of simplicity and versatility. The Pharisees (and some later church traditions) developed an approach to Sabbath that was cluttered, labyrinthine, rigid. "For it is: / Do and do, do and do, / rule on rule, rule on rule; / a little here, a little there" (Isa. 28:10).

The rest of God got lost amid a maze of man-made rules. To recover Sabbath, returning to more rules is hardly an option.

But a golden rule is different. Jesus's so-called golden rule—do unto others what you would have them do unto you—is striking for its simplicity and its versatility. You can memorize it after one or two hearings and apply it lifelong, in virtually every and any situation.

So I submit this as Sabbath's golden rule: *Cease from what is necessary. Embrace that which gives life.*

And then do whatever you want.

Sabbath Liturgy: Practicing the Presence of God

Brother Lawrence as a man, I think, would have left little impression on most of us. Not at first, at least. Maybe not at all. I imagine him meek and small, unobtrusive. I think he had a voice thin as paper, a voice shaped for quiet, bruised by noise. You would have had to hold very still, as with a perching bird, to draw him near. You would have had to bend very close, as with a shy child, to hear him. I think Brother Lawrence was a man other men usually miss, typically dismiss.

Which is too bad. His quietness was thoughtfulness. And in his quietness, Brother Lawrence discovered one of life's deep secrets, and he was happy to tell others about it for the asking: God is everywhere. God hovers in the air just behind you. God slips in, furtive and alert, among your comings and your goings. God listens, and watches, and—yes—speaks. Only, you need to slow down enough to notice. But so often we, like Martha, become distracted by many things and miss Jesus sitting right there in our kitchen.

The devil distracts. God interrupts. And for some reason, we fall prey to the one and grow oblivious to the other. Brother Lawrence found the most simple device for reversing this. In his small, wise book, *The Practice of the Presence of God*, he speaks about a companionship with Jesus that is without boundary—not in time, or place, or circumstance. Anywhere, everywhere, in anything, you can be with God. God wishes it and invites it and is present and available right now for it.

The only thing missing is us. The one thing lacking is attentiveness. So Brother Lawrence commends a discipline—simple as saying hello—of becoming present with God in season and out, in church and away, in crisis and routine, in ecstasy and heartache, in thrill and tedium. In all these things, as Paul says, we are more than conquerors—not because of some swaggering valor in us, but because we have a God to whom we can cry, "Abba" (see Rom. 8:15). We have a God who is there.

How aware have you been, right now, that Jesus is with you? Why don't you greet him, out loud or, if that's awkward for you, in your heart? Even if you are sitting somewhere public—a café, a subway, a city square, a quiet library, a noisy marketplace—do this. I am always amazed at the thrill of homecoming it awakens in me. It is like spotting a trusted friend among a throng of strangers.

In a later chapter and liturgy, we'll explore listening to God. That's not the practice here. This is simply noticing him in order to be with him. It is discovering that what he promised holds true: "Never will I leave you; / never will I forsake you" (Heb. 13:5).

Brother Lawrence washed dishes in a monastery. He was a busboy. He carried out menial duties: tidying and scouring the mess of others, removing the slop and stain of their appetites. But when you sit with him awhile (for that is the effect his book creates), you sense, even amid the clank of plates, the steam of dishpan, the rinds and grease of another's devouring, that he was a king enthroned, a bridegroom on his wedding night, a father holding his newborn. He was the most joyful man in the house.

All because he just kept saying hello.

NINE

PLAY:
Stopping Just to Waste Time

Nathan is twenty-one years old and almost invincible. He seems to think so, at any rate, and I'm inclined to believe him. He is certainly magnificent, if magnificence is measured by gorilla strength and monkey agility, by wild audacity and, maybe, by a touch of harebrained madness.

Nathan jumps off anything. Today, it's a one-hundred-foot cliff, his body straight as a thunderbolt hurled down by Zeus. He sails over a sixty-foot waterfall and lands in a pool churned angry and white by cannonades of water crashing into it. He plunges deep, stays down too long, then pops back up in a boil of frothing water, laughing with joy and a hint of lunacy. You have to laugh too.

A ruined day for Nathan is one that doesn't start by firing his rifle from his house porch, for no better reason than to hear its loud crack in the morning air and smell the sharp scent of gunpowder, and doesn't contain some close brush with the grave. He spends his summers rappelling out of helicopters into burning forests, with no more than an ax, a chain saw, a few other tools. The only water he has is for drinking. His job is to hew down trees outside the fire's perimeter—to cut off its fuel supply—and then to get out before the fire gets him. This isn't work for him. This is play. This is something he'd probably pay to do if he wasn't paid handsomely for doing it. In the winter, he fishes for salmon or king crab off the rocky, stormy coastline of British Columbia, and in deep winter he goes north, Arctic north, to test his wits against its ruthless cold and harrowing loneliness and terrifying emptiness.

To pass the time, he does any number of death-defying things: free climbs, tree climbs, leaps from bridges. His life is a round of cougar chasing, bear baiting, glacier walking.

Most people hope they die in their sleep. They want to go serene, oblivious, slipping into eternity without so much as a toss of the limbs. But dying like that would rob Nathan. If he doesn't die spectacularly, flinging hurdy-gurdy into a hurricane, tumbling headlong from a mountain bluff, getting sucked out to sea in a gnashing riptide, he'll be one spoilsport in heaven. I said that to him once. He looked at me with his impish grin. "Yeah," he said. "A grizzly bear. That would be my pick, torn to shreds tangling with a grizzly bear."

I pity the grizzly.

Anyhow, Nathan wanted me to go swimming with him. Swimming with Nathan is not like swimming with almost anyone else. This will not be a nice little dip in some warm, lazy river. It will not be a splash-and-wade in some park-side lake, with a sandy beach and a dock twenty feet out and a rope held up by oblong floats marking the boundary. There will be no lifeguard sitting nearby, itching to rescue someone.

Nathan swims in rapids. Nathan swims in torrents. Nathan cavorts beneath cataracts. Nathan plunges into icy white water that sluices through narrow gorges and whirls in deep rock bowls. You have to scale down cliffs, clinging to tree roots and grass tufts, even to reach the places Nathan swims. Or, if you're him, you can just jump off the cliff.

No, nothing mild for Nathan. Nothing safe for him. Nothing sane for this boy. Nathan walks out on trees lodged between gorge walls, triple-somersaults into the blue-black water, and lets the plunging current carry him away. Nathan swims in water so muscular and swift, in currents that braid and unravel like large snakes mating, that the water can grip you and spin you round and round until you have no strength except to sink. He swims in eddies that can pin you subsurface on the underside of a ledge and leave you there like a barnacle.

Nathan wanted me to go swimming with him.

I'm middle-aged. My day job involves a lot of sitting. I don't care for heights. I panic in swift water, do all the things you're not supposed to: thrash, fight, swim against the pull of the current. And this was late September, after nearly a month of heavy rains that had brought the river up several feet, dropped its temperature several degrees, and made the river's pools and channels, only a few weeks before safe as a Jacuzzi, now deathly treacherous.

Nathan wanted me to go swimming with him.

The night before our trip, I call Nathan, a bit anxious. "Um, listen: I'm going to live through this, right?"

Long pause. "You know," Nathan says, "I was thinking about that. I was thinking how much the church would hate me if I killed you." Nathan likes to joke, but he's not joking now. He adds nothing to reassure me. It doesn't seem to occur to him that my wife and children might be a tad upset too. He says, "Good night, see you in the morning."

I don't sleep well.

We arrive at the river, and the first things I see, everywhere, are large, bold yellow signs, official signs, all with the same message:

DANGER!
This area is marked by Extreme Danger.
Beware Steep Cliffs
and

Treacherous Waters.
Stay inside the fence.

Unfortunately, this is just a recommendation. Just a suggestion. It's not a command. It has no teeth: violators will not be imprisoned and fined and beaten and shamed. There's no law saying you can't go on the other side of the fence. Only common sense would say that.

Nathan isn't strong on common sense.

I think we are going to start slow, find some gentle, shallow pool and get our feet wet. This is not so. We start by jumping off a thirty-foot bridge into a narrow channel whose current, if you don't catch the edge of rock it rifles past, tosses you off a waterfall. From there we lunge across the current to catch the bank on the other side, then pick our way over a ridge of boulders above a waterfall to leap off a twenty-foot cliff into a frothing spill basin and swim back to the far side.

And just after this I nearly drown.

I swallow water and can't get my breath. I cough and gasp, grasp at a rock shelf to pull myself out. The water keeps pulling me back in. I must look like a cat in bathwater, scrabbling frantically against the hard sides of the tub, getting nowhere. I'm caught in a medicine bowl: a whirlpool that keeps spinning you so that, unless you're strong as Nathan, you're good as dead. I keep going around, still not breathing right. I panic.

"Do you need help?" Nathan calls.

"Yes!"

Next time around the rock wall, just before the current opens out into the wider stream, Nathan reaches out and plucks me up as if I am no more than a newspaper boat bobbing down a street gutter after a heavy downpour.

I sit on the rocks, panting, humiliated. I want to go home. I don't say this, but it's in my heart. Nathan, of course, has other ideas.

"Let's go to the Big Falls," he says.

Yes. Good. The Big Falls.

The Big Falls are, well, big. Very big. They spill in a veil of glittering, thundering water into a pool so deep it could swallow a ship. The waterfall is maybe sixty feet. Above and just behind it, another forty or so feet higher, is a thin shelf atop a sheer column of rock. I pick my way down the cliff into the gorge one hundred feet below, clawing along a narrow, zigzagging footpath. Meanwhile, Nathan positions himself on the ledge above the falls. From where I stand below, he looks small and far away, a bird of prey perched in its aerie. He stands and waits. He isn't hesitating from fear. I'm not sure Nathan knows what fear is. He's getting a line on his landing point. There are rocks under the falls and to the right of them. There's only about a twelve-foot-wide pocket of clear, unobstructed water, where he can plunge sixty feet beneath the surface and not touch bottom. Nathan's aiming for the center of that twelve feet.

And hits it.

More than once.

Meanwhile, I do know what fear is, and I am locked in a fierce contest with it. I know I'd never jump from *that* cliff. I wish only for a small redemption, a modest reclamation of my manhood. I want only enough courage to dive a ten-foot ledge into the pool's twisting, heaving water and survive it. I want only to get in and get out again alive and to do it with some dignity, without feeling like a spindly limbed old man or a sapling-limbed young boy, someone in need of rescue.

There's an off-the-cuff remark that Maggie Smith's character makes in the movie *Gosford Park*, an Agathie Christie–style whodunit that depicts the infinite gradations of snobbery among the British aristocracy and their servants. Smith plays Constance Trentham, a grande dame of snootiness. She is majestically haughty and self-absorbed. She never stifles a caustic opinion or barbed remark about anyone and everyone. After Constance has gone on a jag excessive even for her, someone tells her not to be such a snob, to which she retorts, with surprised indignation, "Why, I haven't a snobbish bone in my whole body."

I am thinking about that, listening to the roar of the falls, watching the boiling of the water. I have some good friends, male friends, and we like to think we've given up the myth of machismo. We like to think that we don't need to strut and howl and do dangerous, foolhardy things to feel we're real men. We like to think we don't have some primitive throwback need to prove ourselves, to convince ourselves and our friends and our women and our children that we're steel-nerved and red-blooded. "Why, I haven't a macho bone in my whole body" is our secret motto.

But standing on this rock ledge above this torrent of river, I know I am soaked to the gills with it. I need to prove this to myself. To Nathan. To my wife and son and two daughters. To the crowd that has gathered atop the cliff, leaning in against the steel-mesh fence, to gawk at Nathan's antics. To everyone who will later hear me crow about it—or will come to my graveside and grieve the glory of my fallen heroism.

So I dive.

And I live.

And I dive and dive and dive again, and live and live and live.

(I told you you'd have to hear me crow about it.)

We went from there to other pools and eddies and falls. Even Nathan got in trouble once: he lassoed a rope to a rock above a short but furious waterfall and pulled himself under the fall's veil to frolic like an otter, leap like a spawning salmon. Only, the undertow was too strong, and it swept him down and pinned him underwater against a rock cavity. I waited and waited for him to come up, wondering what I'd do if he didn't. I knew I didn't have the strength to rescue him. But should I go down there and die with him? Then suddenly he popped up, went down again, and came up once more, gasping, glad to be alive.

That's just it: we were both glad to be alive. A day like that puts that in you. And more: it makes you *feel* alive, alive in every joint and marrow, alive inside and out. In everything—the food you eat, the people you meet, the trees around you, the conversations you have—in everything, a day like that sharpens your senses. It makes you thankful and amazed. It makes the taste and smell and color and texture of everything intensely vibrant. It heightens the meaning of every last little thing.

And it's not just because you brushed death and escaped. *It's that you tasted life and came back for more.* It's that you did something for no reason other than the sheer pleasure of doing it.

I wrestled with whether to go at all. It wasn't just my fear of death that gave me pause. It was also, and mainly, my fear of a deadline: I had to get this book written and had carefully allotted the time I had to do it, assigning myself daily and weekly word quotas.

How ironic. This book is about rest. It's about breaking our captivity to *chronos*, about learning to live free of taskmasters. It's about changing our minds, thinking in new ways about rest and play. It's about God becoming bigger and us becoming smaller. It's about rediscovering simplicity and earthiness and wonder.

And I almost missed it. I almost allowed my obligation to write about rest steal my experience of it. I almost allowed my compulsion to merely talk about rest and play take from me these things themselves.

Enough about swimming gorges. As they say in those truck commercials, don't try this at home.

But do you play enough? Do you risk enough and bask in God's creation enough and do some things for no reason other than that you'll be dead soon enough anyhow, so why not live a little now?

If there's one god of the age that Christians especially pay homage to, it's the god of utility. As a tribe, we're deeply, devoutly utilitarian. Everything we do we seek to justify on the grounds of its usefulness. I took part once in a discussion with pastors about whether or not we should watch movies. One group argued that movies were the idiom and medium of our culture, and that failing to keep abreast of the most influential ones was akin to a missionary's refusing to learn the local dialect and customs, robbing us of the very tools we needed to reach our neighbors. That sounded right. The other group, though, argued that movies were the culture's primary embodiments and carriers of its godlessness, and exposure to them was akin to a missionary's participating in the local voodoo or witch doctor rituals, robbing us of the very authority we needed to reach our neighbors. That sounded right too.

But afterward, I realized that both groups were arguing their opposite views from what amounted to a single position: utilitarianism. Each group wanted to justify their view on the grounds of its usefulness. Either watching movies made us more shrewd, or it made us less holy. It increased our effectiveness or hampered it. It enhanced our influence or diminished it.

It made us more useful or less so.

What's missing is a theology of play. There are many things—eating ice cream, diving off cliffs, sleeping in Saturday mornings, learning birdcalls, watching movies—that can't be shoehorned into a utilitarian scheme, try as you might. We do some things just for the simple sake of doing them. There's no particular usefulness connected with them. They don't *need* to be done: nobody insists, and the world's left unchanged by our doing them or not. They add nothing to the gross national product. They enhance our intellect not one bit. They don't make us worse or better neighbors. They don't improve our figures, hone our skills, or increase our red blood cell counts—or if they do, it's sheer accident, not the thing we set out to accomplish. Accomplishment is the least of their concerns.

But they just might make us feel more alive, more ourselves, and that's use enough. Indeed, many other uses might follow after this. But I want to make something very clear: though play benefits us, the minute we do it for its benefit is the minute it ceases to be play. Play is subversive, really. It subverts business as usual. It subverts necessity. It subverts utility. It subverts all the *chronos*-driven, taskmaster-supervised, legalism-steeped activities that mark out most of our lives—that make us oh-so-useful, but bland and sullen in our usefulness.

Sabbath is for play. I've talked to people who grew up in strict Sabbatarian homes who were forbidden to play on the Sabbath. They couldn't toss or kick or whack a ball, ride a bike, run. They certainly couldn't play rummy or Monopoly. All diversion was out of bounds. Some tell me of sitting in starchy clothes, in a house preternaturally quiet, so quiet you could hear the clock ticking, the floor joists creaking, the fly tapping the windowpane. They gazed out that window, at sunlight soaking spring leaves radiantly, or wind tossing fall leaves kaleidoscopically, or thick flakes of snow swirling down on dark, stripped branches, and they ached to be out there and resented that they couldn't.

This is odd, that we ever emptied Sabbath of play. I grew up in a home with no religious influence, so I have no inkling about how those who ran these Sabbatarian homes thought. But my guess is that they were beholden to the grimmest form of utilitarianism. My guess is that they figured since we spend six days in unbroken usefulness, we should spend one in unbroken restfulness. My guess is that rest was the only alternative they could imagine to work.

But what about play? What about spending some of the day in sheer, unapologetic *uselessness*—not just ceasing from our utilitarian existence, but turning it right on its head? What about spending time producing nothing but adrenaline, laughter, memories?

In C. S. Lewis's classic *The Lion, the Witch and the Wardrobe*, the two girls Susan and Lucy witness the terror and sorrow of Aslan's death at the hands of the White Witch and her henchmen. And then they witness his resurrection. The first thing Aslan does? He plays:

> "Oh, children," said the Lion, "I feel my strength coming back to me. Oh, children, catch me if you can!" He stood for a second, his eyes very bright, his limbs quivering, lashing himself

> with his tail. Then he made a leap high over their heads and landed on the other side of the Table. Laughing, though she didn't know why, Lucy scrambled over it to reach him. Aslan leaped again. A mad chase began. Round and round the hilltop he led them, now hopelessly out of their reach, now letting them almost catch his tail, now diving between them, now tossing them in the air with his huge and beautifully velveted paws and catching them again, and now stopping unexpectedly so that all three of them rolled over together in a happy laughing heap of fur and arms and legs. It was such a romp as no one has ever had except in Narnia; and whether it was more like playing with a thunderstorm or playing with a kitten Lucy could never make up her mind. And the funny thing was that when all three finally lay together panting in the sun the girls no longer felt in the least tired or hungry or thirsty.[1]

Whether it was more like playing with a thunderstorm or playing with a kitten Lucy could never make up her mind.

Both play and Sabbath participate in something outside the bounds of strict utility and chronology. They dance in a woods unwatched by Chronos, outside his repressive rule. Play is the forest of Nottingham, where the sheriff fears to tread. A game is not played on strictly chronological time scales: it's played according to its own logic—innings, rounds, sets, quarters, periods. You play until you're finished. Swimming with Nathan is the same: you go until you're tired, or you drown.

But play is also subversive. It hints at a world beyond us. It carries a rumor of eternity, news from a kingdom where Chronos and utility are no more welcome than death and Hades and the ancient serpent. When we play, we nudge the border of forever.

And this also is what happens when we keep Sabbath. Sabbath, Abraham Joshua Heschel says, is a foretaste and a heralding of eternity. Its joy is precisely this: it rehearses heaven.[2] This, too, is what the writer of Hebrews says—in a passage we'll look at closely in a later chapter: the rest we experience in Sabbath is only preliminary. It is an anticipation, as shadow is of reality, of a rest that never ends.

Play and Sabbath are joined at the hip, and sometimes we rest best when we play hardest. Whether it's more like playing with a thunderstorm or playing with a kitten, you can never make up your mind.

And if you're ever on Vancouver Island and feel like swimming, I know just the place.

Sabbath Liturgy:
Game Plan

Adulthood is mostly about getting things done. Past a certain age, our existence is consumed by obligation. Deadlines loom. Assignments are due. Responsibilities are mountainous. Chores are piling up. There's a list, always, of things to do. Accomplishing these things yesterday has virtually no bearing on our performance of them again today. Or tomorrow. Let up for more than, say, forty-eight hours, seventy-two at the outside, and the world begins to teeter.

So one of the first things to die in adults is playfulness. We are, as a tribe, a grim bunch generally: stern and mirthless, bent beneath huge, invisible weights. Most grown-ups—and an increasing number of youth and children—feel that life is all work and no play. Play feels irresponsible. How can you justify it when there are so many things still to do on your to-do list? How can you feel guiltless in it when the chores you neglected last week are now added to the chores you've yet to attend to this week?

And *you* want to go golfing?

Of all the things Jesus meant when he exhorted his disciples to be childlike, few dare to suggest he wanted them to play more. But maybe he did. Maybe all the other virtues of childhood—trust, humility, simplicity, innocence, wonder—are not separate from a life of playfulness, but the fruit of it: that apart from cartwheels and kite flying, leapfrog and hide-and-seek, snakes-and-ladders and digging for buried treasure, all those other things wither.

Certainly, this: the death of play spells the conquest of Chronos. When we really believe that we have *no time to waste*—no time simply to enjoy without excuse or guilt, without having to show anything for it—then the cult of utility is utterly ascendant. It has vanquished all rivals.

Do you want to hand the god of utility that much territory? Isn't there still, stirring somewhere inside you, a streak of defiance? Isn't there at least the faint pulse of subversion?

When last did you take a day just to play? Or even an hour? Half an hour? When did you last initiate a game with your children and not much care about what time the clock said? Some grown-ups have neglected play so long, they've lost all instinct, all reflex, all capacity for it. Maybe you're one of them. Start slow. Try a card game, or saddle yourself up on a park swing and see how high you can go. Read a book different from this one: a twisty-turny thriller, or a fluffy romance. Or a comic book. Watch a Monty Python movie, or an old Peter Sellers one.

Dance.

In the movie *Patch Adams*, Robin Williams is a medical student who has every bit as much acumen and skill as any of his classmates. But he also has something they don't: a riotous sense of humor and a childlike love of play. Patch treats his patients—some with terrible, crushing illnesses, some victims of accidents that have left them shattered in mind and body—with the medicine, not just of pharmaceuticals, but of laughter. He comes to their bedsides dressed as a clown, or with Groucho glasses, and goes through his routine with slapstick antics reminiscent of Laurel and Hardy. His classmates, one in particular, disdain him for this.

But never mind that. There *is* healing in that laughter, not least of all for the one who brings it.

TEN

RESTORE:
Stopping to Become Whole

After fifteen years of pastoral ministry, I rested.

I took a sabbatical. In fact, I'm on it now, as I write. By the time you read this, though, the sabbatical will be long gone, a fossil of memory faint as ancient fish bones pressed into hardened mud. But for now, I have several months to step back, breathe, stretch, ponder. I can spend an entire day reading if I choose. I can browse a used bookstore at my leisure or shave cedar stumps into thin sticks of kindling even though I have boxes of it already. I can spend uninterrupted hours handpicking words, hand-sculpting sentences. I can nap midday if the mood hits me or go for a walk or sort old paint cans.

There's a country lane not far from me, lined with oak and chestnut trees, and this time of year I can collect handfuls of chestnuts as lustrous as jewels, bagfuls of acorns capped with perfect little cross-hatched tams, and heap them in glass bowls just to be looked at. When a car passes by this stretch of road, this wind-fallen treasure snaps and pops beneath its tires like strings of firecrackers set off all at once.

Or I can drive to a place where the tide has scooped out the earth from the roots of huge bent maple and fir and arbutus trees and crawl through them as if they're mazes in a medieval gauntlet. I can drive to another place where the pounding of the waves has smoothed the stones flat and round like old Roman coins, perfect for skipping if the surf weren't always in such tumult.

I've been looking forward to this for a long time. For years, in fact. It's not that I don't enjoy what I do—I love it most days, except Mondays, and sometimes Wednesdays, and every Thursday afternoon when the sermon still feels rough-cut and patchwork. But all the rest of the time I love it. Actually, that's the problem: I love it overmuch. I spend an average amount of time doing my work, fifty or so hours a week. No more, maybe a tad less, than most people at their jobs. But then I spend many more hours thinking about my work, talking about it, stewing over it, jotting memos to myself concerning it. I'll lie down in bed and remember some odd Greek word I want to look up or think up some new slant on a conversation I should therefore resume, and I'll spring out of bed and shuffle downstairs to scrawl something in a journal or rummage a scrap note from a haystack of paper.

In a word, I'm obsessed.

This is good some days, but most days it's not. It produces the complete reversal of what I intend. I intend to do my work with excellence. I intend to solve problems diligently, preach fervently, care compassionately. I intend to be heartfelt and skillful in the things to which I put my hand. But I sometimes end up with none of that. I end up withered. I spark with dry static. When I'm really tired, I get mildly paranoid. I suspect conspiracies afoot. I start to distrust people. I resent interruptions. I stop caring. I become a master of diversions. I get sloppy and cagey and prickly and forgetful. I clench my jaw too much, which gives me headaches, which make me irritable. I winch tight my shoulders, as if I'm poising to batter-ram open a door in the manner of an old-style cop, which makes the muscles along my neck and back rigid and spasmodic.

So a sabbatical started to look like a good idea.

About a year before I took it, I was invited to speak to a group of pastors in a neighboring city. I gave my speech, and the host opened the floor for questions. Someone asked me what he should do on a sabbatical. I told him I hadn't a clue, that I'd love to find out, and could he please arrange to speak to my board? They laughed, politely. Then this thought came to me: "I don't think it's possible to benefit from a sabbatical if you've never learned to keep Sabbath. Sabbatical is Sabbath writ large. If we haven't been faithful in the small things, why do we expect to be entrusted with the greater ones? I see a lot of people head toward a sabbatical like it's the great white hope, a supercure, the answer to all that ails them, and then come out of it sorely disappointed. They emerge more tired than when they went in.

"Sabbatical is just doing daily, for several months of days, what you've already learned to do weekly, for many years of weeks."

It sounded wise at the moment. Even borderline profound.

It haunts me now. It's not that I'm off to a bad start. It's just that now I get to test the soundness of my claim. If this is a good season for me, it will be because I already know the rest of God.

As I left for sabbatical, many people in my church wished me well. They told me they'd miss me, that they'd be praying for me, that they hoped I came back refreshed. And then they usually said, "You deserve this."

I don't. I can think of all kinds of people who deserve it: a single mother who works three jobs to ensure her kids have a decent home and good clothes; a couple who have been clocking twelve-hour days or more six days a week for many years, trying to keep a small business from sliding over the edge; a tradesman who never has time for a holiday when the work is on and never has money for one when it's not; a millworker whose shifts change like the clouds so that he's seen the inside and out of every hour of every day and now never quite sleeps and never fully wakes. I can think of all the people who do their jobs faithfully and capably, even though they die at it a little every day. I like what I do, and I have not worked half as hard as half of these people, and few will ever be given the luxury of a sabbatical.

No, I don't deserve it. It's pure gift, like being born in peacetime and not war, like being forgiven, or kissed, or told you have beautiful eyes. I never earned a minute of it. I don't deserve a scrap of it.

But I feel deeply obliged to the people in my church who have allowed me it. Obliged, not to come back smarter, or thinner, or more eloquent, or more studied up, though all that could help. The obligation I feel is *not* to pay them back. These things don't work that way, on some barter system where the church trades several months of leave in exchange for shorter, pithier sermons.

The obligation I feel, rather, is to come back restored.

It's not that I went out maimed, not really. There was another time, a few years ago, that if the door of sabbatical had been opened, I would have hobbled out and spent the time given just trying to piece myself back together, trying to find some dim, quiet room where the light didn't sting my eyes and no loud noises startled me. But the door wasn't opened then. I managed anyhow. This time, the time I was handed a sabbatical, I went out sprightly, still swinging, still singing.

Still, I feel I owe it to the church to come back restored.

I had better explain.

Jesus defied the Sabbath conventions of his day. The scribes and Pharisees, like Delilah, kept trying to bind him up in elaborate snares, and Jesus, like Samson, kept throwing off the bindings with ease and disdain, as though so much singed thread. Here's a man in the synagogue with a shriveled hand, lying directly in front of Jesus. They watch. Will Jesus flout their Sabbath regulations and heal him?

He does.

Here's a woman shuffling her way into the meeting place, her shoulders a mound of skewed bone and twisted sinew. They watch. Will Jesus affront their dignity, brook their growing disapproval, and heal her?

He will.

These stories, like courtroom dramas, ooze with political intrigue. They crackle with caustic dialogue and bristle with sharp-edged retort. They're spellbinding yarns. But what we sometimes miss is the human story.

The man. His hand a gift he never treasured until he lost it. One day he suffered an injury or an illness—a large stone lodged in the teeth of a harrow, maybe, and he reached down to pull it out, and the oxen lurched, and the hand was caught and mangled on the spikes. Or a cut on his arm, just a nick, really, got dirt in it, and two days later the wound erupted in a mess of pus and rawness. The infection throbbed down into nerve and marrow, and that hand crumpled in on itself and never came back. Or it could have been any number of things.

Now he hauls that hand around like a dense burl of wood he picked up to burn, like a fish he bought at the market to boil, cold and stiff with death. Only he can't put it down, not ever. He's had to develop all kinds of techniques for getting around it, to compensate for the absence of his hand's use, the presence of its uselessness. A whole half of his body has grown thin and weak doing this, the other half strong and nimble.

There's a man here.

And a woman. For eighteen years she's been like this, stooped and twisted, at war with gravity. Her whole body lists earthward. Who knows how she got this way: Perhaps, turning to say good-bye to a friend, she tripped at the top of stone steps and tumbled to the pavement below, then never really got up again. Or maybe she has some rheumatoid ailment that, with each fresh flare-up, plucks her joints and sockets farther apart, grinds them sharper together, leaves her more misshapen? Jesus recognizes Satan's work here: this has all the hallmarks of his cruelty, his sadism.

Eighteen years, and she still comes to synagogue every Sabbath, hauling her sickness with her. She lugs it on her back, drags it in her hips, hefts it in the soreness and stiffness of her knees. Eighteen years of this, and she still loves God. Maybe she has grandchildren. Maybe her prayers come down to one thing: to have enough straightness in her body, even just once, to hold those children, strong and close and gentle, to pull them into herself and press the wideness of her hands against the birdcages of their ribs.

Jesus sees them. In the midst of his pitched battle with the Pharisees and company, he never misses the man, the woman. He's not just out to prove a point, force an issue, settle a score. This is more than a political showdown for him. This is more than some theological standoff.

These are men and women, real people, with stories and histories, with hopes and sorrows. Jesus sees them, and in that moment of seeing, the other issues at hand dissolve. Jesus becomes single-minded in his purpose: he means to restore.

A curious thing about restoration is that it doesn't need doing. Strictly speaking, life carries on without it. Restoration is an invasion of sorts. It's fixing something that's broken, but broken so long it's almost mended. This man, this woman—they've already adapted to their misfortunes, made all the necessary adjustments. Restoration meddles with what they've learned to handle, removes what they've learned to live with, bestows what they've learned to live without. Replacements have been found already, thank you all the same.

These people are doing fine just the way they are. They've learned to live this way. They've almost accepted it. They've taught themselves tricks to bypass it, to contain it. To utilize it, even. They've built lives around not being whole. They've learned, if not to welcome, at least not to spurn those things their sickness drags in with it. They've learned not to mourn the absence of those things it chases away. Secretly, perhaps, they have come to love their illness.

Sickness can actually steal the place of God. It can become the sick person's center, the touchstone by which he defines himself. Illness is a tyrant with huge territorial ambitions. It is a seductress with large designs. It wants not only the sick person's body. It wants his heart and mind also. It wants to be his all-consuming passion.

No wonder Jesus once asked a man he meant to heal, "Do you want to get well?" (John 5:6). Maybe the man didn't, strange as it sounds. Maybe his sickness had become his haven, his lover, his overlord. And no wonder Jesus was so responsive to any old beggar or leper or blind man who threw caution to the wind and outright begged for healing.

Not everyone wants to get well.

It's the most natural thing to befriend your sickness, even, after long association, to depend upon it. Imagine any of the people Jesus heals. Their entire lives—their physical lives, for sure, but also their emotional and intellectual and relational lives—all have taken shape around their injuries or diseases. That man at the pool of Bethesda whom Jesus first asks if he wants to get well, for instance.

He's been there thirty-eight years. His entire existence has narrowed down to the daily drama of his lifelong suffering: the sores on his undersides, the ghostly sensations flitting along his nerves. He likely has a fermenting resentment toward those whose lot seems a margin better than his own, and a smug disdain toward those whose lot appears slightly worse. At night, sleeping on some narrow cot, he must dream of this place, its people, its shapes, its textures: the old man, rotund and dewlapped, stretched across the wet stones, muttering and shaking his heavy jowls; the young girl, rawboned and waxy skinned, with a voice faint as a handrubbing cloth; the sound when the water churns, like big boulders falling at a distance; the sudden billowing at the pool's surface, an eruption of froth and steam, and the tumult of bodies heaving, flailing, lurching, as each rushes to find a place before the others do.

Thirty-eight years of monotony. Thirty-eight years of futility. Thirty-eight years of self-pity. Thirty-eight years of poisonous envy and secret pride. Thirty-eight years of never being able to work, travel, make love, cook, care for children, or fix an oxcart. Thirty-eight years of life without options. Thirty-eight years of life without obligations. He carries burdens, yes, but one he's never carried is the weight of others' expectations.

For thirty-eight years.

And then Jesus shows up one day and changes all that. One word from Jesus, and all thirty-eight years fall behind the man, vanish in a blink, and a future he stopped daring to imagine stands vivid and solid before him. He can do all the things he never could and ever wanted to do. He can do them here and now—for Jesus's miracle joins healing and therapy in one terse command. Muscles spongy from years of idleness suddenly grow taut and supple. Bones spindly from never bearing the body's full weight turn instantly thick and sturdy. Balance all topsy-turvy from chronic proneness immediately calibrates for walking, running, dancing, leaping.

And now the man can work and pay taxes. And now he can marry and take on domestic responsibilities. And now he can build a home and fix its roof when it leaks and shim the door when it skews crooked. And now he relinquishes the unique status suffering bestows on a man and enters the anonymity that comes with being well. Now he loses the strange privilege of sickness and takes up the everyday obligations of health. He's just like everybody else now. We expect things of him.

Do you want to get well?

Restoration shocks the system. It alters not just our health—it alters our world. All that we establish to placate or indulge or accommodate our sickness disintegrates with those stark words, "Take up your mat, and go."

Do you want to get well?

Do *I* want to get well? That's a question I've wrestled with on sabbatical. If I believe I'm to go back restored, in what ways am I sick now? And how have I grown content with that?

I try to control too much, is one. I know how this happened—there was a season when the church seemed to require it. There was a time it seemed that to be at the center of all decision making was the shape strong leadership took. But even if that's so, explanation is no excuse, and the reality is that now I meddle in too many things. And there must be something in me, some flaw, some weakness, that rises to meet the challenge in just this way. Other pastors I know have, in the face of many demands, committed the opposite sin: they've become dangerously passive. My sickness manifests as control. So it's one area where I seek restoration.

I want to return to my work slow to speak, quick to listen, slow to become angry. I want to hide more things in my heart and ponder them there. I want to return with a sharper instinct to pray, to watch and wait, and with less impulsiveness to act straightaway. I want a stronger conviction that, though God welcomes my honest efforts, he manages quite fine without my Peter-like outbursts of ill-conceived enthusiasm and then sudden loss of nerve, my opinion swapping and bully tactics, my reckless volunteerism to fix things for God and then desperate evacuation when things go wrong.

Part of Jesus's regimen for me, I've discovered, is holding my tongue. This is easier right now, during these months, because I'm in daily contact with fewer people—my family, mostly—and they actually require an opinion about or even need my hand in few things. It's something of a shock, realizing how much my family has its own culture and economy—preparing meals, washing walls, shopping for groceries and gym shoes and mouthwash, practicing piano, playing games after school, visiting friends—that I've been pretty much oblivious to and that exists independent of my coming and going. I observe this now with wonder, admiration, some guilt.

So I hold my tongue and realize how the world hums right along without my commentary on it. It manages just fine without my managing of it. It doesn't just survive without me: it—could this be?—appears to do a little better, even, without my incessant tinkering.

There is a deeper lesson here. God is teaching me quietness of heart. I didn't realize, until I started experiencing this, how clamorous and anxious my heart generally is. Inside, I'm a schemer. A constant chattering goes on in my head. I mutter to myself like Gollum. But as I quiet down, my heart does as well. Quietness allows room for God to speak or to be silent. Both are gifts. Quietness stops crowding the Holy Spirit, elbowing aside God's gentle presence. The end of striving makes room for dwelling.

Which leads to another thing. I long to get back to a place I was at a few years ago, where every day I heard God. I was more vigilant then, I think, more expectant and hungry. I was the hunter hunted. I was the man in the woods who depended on the keenness of his senses in order to eat and not be eaten. My pursuit of God had an end-of-the-world kind of desperation. Like Rachel crying to Jacob, "Give me children or I die," I cried to God, "Give me your Spirit or I die." I was spiritually lean, wily, stealthy, alert, and yet also vulnerable, wide open. A child and warrior both.

Somewhere I got dull. The child got old, the warrior timid. Again, I think I know how this happened—a combination of growing responsibility and increased privilege—but so what? Somewhere, I started to play things safe. I started to fall back on tried, tired methods of doing things and stopped asking God each day whether I should fight or not fight, go up or go down. I got formulaic in my thinking. I got hidebound in my routines. In the spring, when kings go out to war, I started to stay home, wander bored and restless on the palace roof, looking for something to make me feel young again.

Do I want to get well?

Yes.

I think.

Sort of.

Maybe.

I'm not sure.

The problem here is that nakedness and hunger are painful. They are like an unclosed wound. And God is relentless, always pressing that wound. He is always calling us higher up the mountain, deeper down in the valley, farther out on the water. And some days, I just want life to be easier. My wife said to me awhile back, "Sometimes I want a holiday from the burden of being made holy. A little time off from God." Or as my daughter Sarah asked when she was four, "Is it true God sees us all the time? Even in our hearts? Even what we're thinking?"

"Yes."

"Oh," she said and looked stricken.

And yet my response is the same as Peter's when Jesus asked his disciples if they, like so many others, wanted to leave him: "Lord, to whom shall we go? You have the words of eternal life" (John 6:68).

I have nowhere else to go.

Yes, I want to get well.

But you don't need a sabbatical for God to restore you, or else most everyone's in trouble.

Sabbath will do.

Jesus's favorite day to heal and restore was the Sabbath. He deemed that day most appropriate. "Should not this woman, a daughter of Abraham, whom Satan has kept bound for eighteen long years, be set free on the Sabbath day from what bound her?" Jesus asks his critics, who think this kind of healing is better done midweek, along with the laundry and hay baling and stone quarrying (Luke 13:16).

Eighteen *long* years. Jesus says that, uses that adjective: *long*. He knew. A year in captivity is longer—darker, bleaker—than a year in freedom. A year in sickness is painstakingly slow, each day an ordeal.

So Jesus isn't working, he's liberating. That's his language too. "Woman," he announces, "you are set *free* from your infirmity" (Luke 13:12, emphasis mine). The religious rulers accuse Jesus of working here, but this woman is the one who's been working. She's had to slave without ceasing beneath her affliction. She's the one cursed liked Sisyphus to this unending toil, only instead of pushing a boulder, she's hauling one. It's on her back. What Jesus does has nothing to do with work as it's commonly conceived.

He sets her free. He liberates her.

Liberation is dangerous. It's costly. It's high drama and high stakes. It calls for enormous risk, superhuman effort, steely nerves. There's an enemy in the way, a vicious enemy, heavily armed, not to be trifled with. Of all the words we might use to describe what Jesus does here, *work* isn't one of them.

Setting free isn't work.

But being set free can be.

You have to want to get well.

U.S. News & World Report featured, on the eve of 2004, a series of articles about people to watch in the coming year and beyond. One was Cynthia Kenyon, a researcher at the University of California whose specialty is the genetic makeup of worms. Cynthia might have spent her entire life in the obscurity of her lab work, rummaging through the molecular intricacies of creepy crawlers, except she stumbled on an astonishing discovery: the gene in worms that turns off—or significantly dials down—the aging process. Daf-2 is the switch, a tiny protein factory that generates the equivalent of insulin.

In 1993, when she first discovered this, she and her team were able to double the life span of a single worm. In late 2003, they increased a worm's life span sixfold, the equivalent of five hundred human years. She's moved her research to mice, with promising though not quite as stunning results. Cynthia's hope—in her own lifetime, of course—is to develop a therapy for humans. "If our company could make a pill," she says, meaning a pill that dramatically extends longevity, "everyone would want it."

"I want," Cynthia adds, "to take the pill."[1]

I'm not sure everyone wants it. I don't. It strikes me that, of all the ways God wants to restore us, keeping us earthbound for centuries, genetically altered to live longer lives but otherwise stuck as our same ragged and haggard selves, isn't one of them.

I'm having enough trouble, in these three score and ten years or so I've been allotted, just staying well. I'm struggling as it is to become and remain and grow as a man after God's own heart.

I don't want to live twice as long, or six times that. It is enough, a simple and sufficient prayer, for Jesus just to make me whole.

Sabbath Liturgy:
Wanting to Get Well

A person with a terminal illness is a study in hope. The death sentence handed him becomes, in most cases, an impetus to life. He starts fighting hard, digging in, refusing to be shaken off with pat answers and red tape and gloomy verdicts. He finds ways to dismantle bureaucratic stone walls, to end-run endless committees. He jumps queues and crashes lines. He finagles backdoor access to specialists. If there is a treatment available somewhere—Switzerland, Mexico, New Zealand—he devises a way to get there. If there is some untested or unconventional product available, he makes almost black-market deals to procure it.

This doesn't surprise me. I might, I reckon, do the same if I or someone I loved was diagnosed with such an illness.

What surprises me is how this impulse rarely carries over into the spiritual. The impulse is stirred, deep and strong, when our physical well-being or survival is threatened. But when it has to do with our spiritual well-being—when we are faced with chronic, perhaps terminal, sickness of heart—it hardly flickers.

Physical sickness we usually defy.

Soul sickness we often resign ourselves to.

A woman whose gossip has irreparably damaged every relationship she's had? She usually looks for one more person to whom she can tell the *real* story. A man whose soul has been parched for ten years, who maintains his religious commitments out of dull habit or vague guilt? He is often content in his misery. A teenager whose waywardness is destroying everything he once cherished? He typically looks for someone to blame.

Do you want to get well?

A good Sabbath Liturgy is to take stock. It is to sit and reckon where you are spiritually and calculate the gap between that and where you want to be—or, at least, where you know you ought to want to be. Do you want more grace, or trust, or peace? Do you want a greater sense of God's presence and goodness? Do you want to live by Paul's exhortation in Ephesians 4:29, to "not let any unwholesome talk proceed out of your mouths, but only what is helpful for building others up according to their needs, that it may benefit those who listen"?

We've yet to find a cure for cancer or Crohn's disease or the common cold. But we have discovered the cure for our souls. It may not come easy, but it is free for the asking and available everywhere.

But it begins with an honest answer to that question, *Do I want to get well?*

I have a friend who not long ago phoned a former pastor to apologize to him. My friend had been taking stock and was gripped by a conviction that years before he had failed this pastor. He had not supported him as Scripture commands. He had refused to speak words of life and instead had stood aloof, silent in judgment. He saw how his failure had cost both of them. He also believed that any future effectiveness in his own ministry, and maybe in this pastor's, was tied to his willingness to humble himself and seek forgiveness and make amends.

He wanted to get well.

My friend did as God told him. He called the pastor and, without excuse, apologized. He simply walked in unquestioning obedience to his conviction. Out of that is blossoming for him a long season of fruitfulness and influence.

Recently, God confirmed a call in his own life to become a pastor. My prediction: he'll be a good one.

ELEVEN

FEAST:
Stopping to Taste the Kingdom

I never liked the Tilt-a-Whirl or Whirligig, whatever it's called—that thing at the carnival that spins you round and round, so that you stagger afterward like a man drunk and blind both. The ground slithers beneath you, the sky twists above. It has disks that whirl clockwise within a larger disk that whirls counterclockwise, and the whole thing pitches and heaves worse than a dingy in a hurricane. It's like a torture implement from the Middle Ages, one of those things with pulleys and levers, with ropes and manacles and great, cogged wooden gears. It's a thing barbaric and exquisite all at once, operated by a fat man grown bored in his sadism. It makes me queasy just to watch. I did watch it once, and it convinced me, as though I needed convincing, never to go near it.

This one was called the Mad Hatter. You wedged in five or so people on a circular bench molded inside a giant teacup. The teacup swiveled on its dish, and the dish swiveled on its base, and the base turned and tilted wildly. I watched a group of four girls go on it and sit together in a single teacup. They were strapped in snug to the hard seats, and the machine started up, slow at first. Then, with a jerk, the teacups began to back-eddy. Everyone yelped. The whole awful contraption built up speed and flung the riders faster and faster, forever faster, in wide, dizzying circles. Their screams scattered windward with the motion.

One of the girls wasn't doing well. Her face was taut with anxiety, her eyes shut. She gripped the handlebars in front of her with a death clutch and pushed her body close into the seat. The other girls around her were oblivious, laughing at each swoop and whoosh of the ride, tilting their heads out so their hair whipped hard in the wind. Every time their teacup spun into view, the scene was the same, only a bit worse: the laughing girls with their fanfare of hair, and their horrified, mortified companion. First her face was flushed red. Then blanched white. Then shaded green.

And then she threw up: a great sparkling arc of spew that gushed upward and boomeranged backward and spattered the inside of the teacup like those paintings you could do in another part of the carnival, where you dropped gobs of bright acrylic into a vortex that flung the paint in stringy spatters onto a canvas and you came away with something that looked like one of the works of Jackson Pollock.

But this was no artwork.

This was rock opera. This was Roman carnival. This was *The Rocky Horror Picture Show*, in 3-D. This was enough gore to cure you of cheap thrills for several lifetimes.

The girls stopped laughing, abruptly.

I had to turn away.

That happened a long time ago, but I've never forgotten it. I wish I could. It's become a kind of metaphor for me, that Whirligig, that Mad Hatter. It's become a symbol of the power of amusement to make us sick. Pleasure can be like that: a thing that spins you round and round, faster and faster. Some people enjoy it immensely, at least for short bursts.

They lean into it.

Others aren't doing so well.

Of all the ways our culture spins us dizzy, its obsession with food is one of the most glaring.

Honestly.

We are a Mad Hatter culture, a nation of gluttons and weight-watchers. Go into any gas station food mart, and see for yourself. Magazines, rafts of them, depict men and women with bodies of impossible tautness and hardness and litheness. The women are svelte and buxom, with incandescent skin. They gaze out at you, brazen as harlots or coy as schoolgirls. The men are stone-faced, all of them, grim as though bent on some mortal quest, their bare stomachs an armor plate of muscle, their arms all sinew and veins.

These pictures are arrayed next to shelves laden with chocolate bars, tubs of candies, shrink-wrapped trays of mini-donuts, racks bulging with bags of chips and cheesies and nachos, walls of refrigerators stuffed full with creamy and sugary drinks. And that's not all. Beside the magazines with our pantheon of beautiful people are other magazines, magazines that have on their covers photos of succulent, sweet-drenched desserts, casseroles dense with sauces and sausage and cheese, or mounds of pasta tossed in a rich cream sauce bejeweled with shrimp and scallops. "Details on page 70," the cover announces. Invariably, somewhere on the same cover, in an inset on the top right-hand corner, maybe, is a picture of a woman in a tight dress or skimpy bikini—and she does it justice—with a caption beneath: "How to lose 10 pounds and rid yourself of unsightly cellulite before the beach weather hits! Page 73."

Go up to pay for it, and there at the counter, next to the till, are several paperbacks on various diet fads, and usually a few dessert cookbooks, next to baskets bristling with chocolate treats.

We're a culture stuck between Barbie and the bulge. We dream thin and live fat. We spin this way, spin that way, back and forth, round and round.

Some of us aren't doing so well.

Sabbath is for feasting.

Only I'm not sure that means much anymore. We feast all the time. Which is ironic. Sabbath is often corrupted because we carry into it our weekday, workaday preoccupations. We don't stop. We keep working, keep toiling, and even when we cease from that physically, we carry in our minds a constant nattering. So Sabbath gets stained by the rest of the week.

With food, this staining, this corrupting, goes the opposite direction. We feast like Sabbath-keepers most days, indiscriminately, and so feasting on the Sabbath has lost much of its richness. It's just one more big meal. We eat ourselves stuffed daily. There's nothing to anticipate, nothing to make us stand back, astonished and thankful. "Without a fast," Dorothy Bass writes, "it's hard to recognize a feast."[1] Overabundance is our common lot, muchness our birthright, and all Sabbath serves up is more of the same. And when we see anything as birthright, it ceases to be gift.

It used to bother me that the church had taken the Eucharist—the love feast—and reduced it to such meager portions. What had originally been a visible, bountiful demonstration of the banquet of grace had become, over the centuries, a token of scarcity: a mere crumb of bread, a single mouthful of wine or juice. But I wonder if, rather than scarcity, the meal now symbolizes simplicity. In a gluttonous age, where nothing is enough, the sparseness of the Communion meal becomes a reminder that grace is sufficient, that our daily bread is all we need.

At any rate, one of the disciplines of Sabbath-keeping for our age is to practice a deeper frugality the other six days.

I usually eat cold cereal in the morning. That seems frugal enough, ascetic even. But recently my wife bought new breakfast bowls to replace the plastic children's bowls with pictures of Buzz Lightyear painted on the inside. The new bowls are much bigger than the old ones. They're about twice the size, in fact. I filled it up. What good is a half-filled bowl? If God led a bowl maker to make a bowl that wide and that deep—with that much capacity—it must have been for a reason. So I filled it up.

At first, the extra helping hurt. I could hardly swallow those last few spoonfuls, and once or twice I even tossed out the soggy remains. But then I got so I could down it without blinking, and sometimes I even added another shake from the box—to use up the leftover milk, you understand. And then I noticed my appetite increased proportionally for lunch, for dinner, and for snacks between meals.

And then I noticed my pants getting tighter.

So I started to rein myself in. And, of course, I was at first hungry a lot, feeling shortchanged, like Oliver Twist turned away by the churlish soup ladler when all he wanted was a little more.

But I also noticed that the times of real feasting—a dinner we went to recently with good friends, for instance, where I got a jerked halibut, black with hot spice, and a half-plate full of thin, curled French fries—have started to mean more. Moments like that are starting to feel like gifts again, not rights.

I'm starting to enjoy being hungry.

In Deuteronomy, Moses—in a passage that connects with the Ten Commandments and so with the Sabbath—told the people this:

> Remember how the LORD your God led you all the way in the desert these forty years, to humble you and to test you in order to know what was in your heart, whether or not you would keep his commands. He humbled you, *causing you to hunger and then feeding you with manna,* which neither you nor your fathers had known, to teach you that man does not live on bread alone but on every word that comes from the mouth of the LORD. . . .
>
> Observe the commands of the LORD your God, walking in his ways and revering him. For the LORD your God is bringing you into a good land—a land with streams and pools of water, with springs flowing in the valleys and hills; *a land with wheat and barley, vines and fig trees, pomegranates, olive oil and*

> *honey; a land where bread will not be scarce and you will lack nothing. . . .*
>
> When you have eaten and are satisfied, praise the LORD your God for the good land he has given you. Be careful that you do not forget the LORD your God, failing to observe his commands, his laws and his decrees that I am giving you this day. Otherwise, when you eat and are satisfied, . . . then your heart will become proud and you will forget the LORD your God, who brought you out of Egypt, out of the land of slavery. (Deuteronomy 8:2–3, 6–12, 14, emphasis mine)

Be careful when you eat well. Be careful when God lavishes wealth on you so that feasting is your daily experience. Be careful lest you come to expect it. Be careful when those days of testing and refining and humbling and disciplining that hunger brings are long forgotten. Be careful when the days of having to look to God for daily bread and water from the rock are a murky memory, faintly embarrassing.

I don't know how else the memory of hunger can be kept alive except by sometimes being hungry.

Fasting is good for this. But restraint in our eating—the practice of frugality—is good as well. Then, when we interrupt our frugality with feasting—on Sabbath days, wedding days, birthdays, national holidays, and the like—we are like workers in from the harvest. We are soldiers home from war. We are hunters returning.

Some quality of life should mark the difference between our days of rest and celebration and our days of toil and production. Times of indulgence mean nothing if all times are that: always eating, never feasting. But if we reserve our feasting for a few occasions, for holidays and holy days, for times set apart, then each acquires a richer luster, a purer and sweeter tone.

Thomas Costain, in his book *The Three Edwards*, relates a historical episode from the fourteenth century. Two brothers, Raynald and

Edward, fought bitterly. Edward mounted war against Raynald, captured him alive, and imprisoned him in Nieuwkerk Castle.

But it was no ordinary prison cell. The room was reasonably comfortable. And there was no lock on the door—not a bolt, not a padlock, not a crossbeam. Raynald was free to come or go at will. In fact, it was better than that: Edward promised Raynald full restoration of all rights and titles on a single condition: that he walk out of that room.

Only Raynald couldn't. The door was slightly narrower than a typical door. And Raynald was enormously fat. He was swaddled in it. He could not, with all his squeezing and heaving, get himself outside his cell. He might more easily have passed a camel through a needle.

So in order to walk free and reclaim all he'd lost, he had only to do one thing: lose weight. That would have come easily to most prisoners, with their rations of bread and water.

It did not come easy to Raynald. Edward had disguised a great cruelty as an act of generosity. Every day, Edward had Raynald served with the richest, sauciest foods, savory and sweet, and ample ale and wine to boot. Raynald ate and ate and grew larger and larger. He spent ten years trapped in an unlocked cell, freed only after Edward's death. His health was so ruined, he died soon himself.[2]

To reclaim his kingdom, all he had to do was stay hungry.

But there's another food the Bible speaks about. It is not physical food. It is God's will—doing what he asks, finishing the work he sent us to do.

That's the way Jesus put it.

It's high noon on a hot, hot day. Jesus is exhausted, hungry, and thirsty. He sits down to rest on the stone edge of a well, and his men go into town to fetch lunch. And out of the heat-creased air a woman appears. A water pot perches on her shoulder. She's alone. It's an odd time of day for this—why not at sundown, when evening shadows spread their coolness over the land? It's an odd thing that she's by herself—why not with the women from the village, easing the burden of their work with the levity of their friendships?

She comes alone in the heat of the day.

Jesus asks her for help. *Can you give me something to drink?*

The question startles her, on several counts. A man, speaking to a woman. A Jew, speaking to a Samaritan. A holy man, speaking to . . . *her.*

Then Jesus does something that startles her even more. *He offers her water.* "Living water," he calls it: water that so satisfies, so quenches thirst, one sip is enough, forever (John 4:10). She's taken aback and starts an argument about sacred traditions and worship styles and holy sites. A familiar argument.

Jesus reveals many things to her. He tells her that God is looking for worshipers. He lets on that he knows she has lived—indeed, is living—a sinful life. But the most startling revelation is this: he tells her he's the Messiah. She's the first person to whom he reveals this. He hasn't even told his disciples yet.

Jesus chooses these circumstances, this place, this person—his own weariness and thirstiness and hunger, the dusty outskirts of a Samaritan village, a woman who's lived from one broken relationship to the next—to make the announcement.

His disciples return, appalled to find Jesus talking to her, though none of them dare speak that out loud. The woman runs off, amazed that he knows all about her—"everything [she] ever did" is how she puts it (John 4:39)—and more amazed that he loves her anyhow, that he does not withdraw or qualify in some way his promise to her of living water. If anything, his knowing her, knowing everything she ever did, makes him more vulnerable and extravagant with her. More willing to risk and bless and reveal. Many Samaritans, stirred by the woman's testimony, come out to see this man for themselves.

Meanwhile, the disciples have brought food. They urge Jesus to eat some. They left him so bedraggled, so worn down. He had that pallor you get from bone weariness, and that darkness like bruises around the eyes. They were worried. He had let himself be stretched too thin.

Eat, Rabbi. Eat something. We've got chicken soup. We've got matzos. We've got falafel. We've got bagels. Take your pick—but by goodness, eat!

"I have food to eat that you know nothing about" (John 4:32).

Huh? What's this? Did someone bring him food? Was it that woman?

These scenes always have a slightly comical tone to them, like a mild British farce. The bumbling disciples, quickly baffled, given to a flat-footed literalism, and the enigmatic Jesus, waxing metaphoric, trying to coax them into an awareness of things unseen. Only it's like trying to get men wearing blindfolds and work gloves to thread needles.

So Jesus tells them straight up: "My food . . . is to do the will of him who sent me and to finish his work" (John 4:34).

Jesus began tired, hungry, and thirsty. He asked the Samaritan woman for water, but she gave him none. He was spent from the journey, but the woman's needs interrupted his own. His disciples brought him food, but he never took a bite. None of Jesus's physical needs were met, yet he was refreshed, alert. His thirst was quenched, his weariness lifted, his hunger satisfied.

His food was to do God's work.

Work typically depletes us. Food gives us the energy to do our work, and then the work uses up that energy. So we eat again. And we have to work to make the money to buy the food. And so we're caught, without relief, in this cycle: the harder we work, the more we must eat, and the more we eat, the harder we must work. In a sense, work and food are opposites, but they exist in this relationship of mutual dependency. Our work provides our food and uses it up. Our food empowers our work and requires it.

But Jesus speaks of a work that moves in the opposite direction: the more we do it, the fuller we get, and the fuller we get, the more we want to do it. This work *is* food, a thing that nourishes, satisfies, strengthens. We savor it, sit back content from it.

The Samaritan woman said to Jesus when he offered her living water, "Sir, give me this water so that I won't get thirsty and have to keep coming here to draw water" (John 4:15). I say to Jesus, "Sir, give me this work so that I won't get tired and have to keep toiling at things that exhaust me."

That work is to do what God wants. Most days, the work I do—preaching, teaching, writing, exhorting—is exactly that. I believe, with deepest conviction, that this is the work God sent me to do and to finish, and I'm a glutton for it. It feeds my craving. It fills my inmost places. I may go into it weary, hungry, thirsty, but I come out replenished. I cannot number the times I have stood up to speak so empty I'm sure I'll fall over, only to finish ready to slay a thousand Philistines with no more than an ass's jawbone. I begin in weakness and end in strength. I discover all over again that this is exactly what God loves: to make his power perfect in our weakness, to show up in splendor when we show up in faithfulness, obedient but inadequate, trusting but inept, with nothing in our hands but our need for him.

"You feed them," he tells us, when we have hardly enough even to feed ourselves. We give what we have anyway and find afterward that everyone has had his fill. There are even basketfuls remaining.

Sabbath helps reorient us to our work. It is an opportunity to step back far enough from what we do to look at it objectively and ask, *Is this what I was sent to do? Am I on course?*

Is this my food?

Maybe an episode from King David's life brings this most clearly into light.

It's late in David's reign. He's accomplished many things: subdued Israel's enemies, extended her borders, amassed great wealth, built a palace, brought the ark to Jerusalem. And he's failed too. Bathsheba, once Uriah's wife, is now his wife, but at great cost. There are children who have died and children who've gone wayward and children whom he's banished. There are wives who are estranged. There are friends who have become, over time, something else: rivals, toadies, parasites, necessary evils.

And then one day, the worst thing of all happens: his son Absalom revolts. Absalom has long nursed royal ambitions and has long been frustrated by his father, David's, refusal to see him. Years earlier, Absalom, angered by his father's inaction, had taken a matter of family honor into his own hands. David had exiled him for his audacity. Later, under the persuasion of his advisers, David allowed Absalom back into Jerusalem, but not back into his presence. The face-to-face encounter was slow in coming.

Somewhere in there, Absalom grows bitter. Somewhere, he sets his sights, not on intimacy with his father, but on something else: deposing him.

So he gathers an army, declares himself king, and lays siege to Jerusalem. David is completely unprepared. He simply beats a hasty retreat, evacuating Jerusalem. Absalom walks in unopposed. As a sign of his conquest over and contempt for his father, and as a seal on his rebellion, he sleeps with David's harem on the palace rooftop, for all the world to see.

And David walks away. He doesn't ride. He is not carried. He walks, unshod and bereft. "David continued up the Mount of Olives, weeping as he went; his head was covered and he was barefoot" (2 Sam. 15:30). As he goes, an old enemy appears. Shimei, one of Saul's kin, bitter from years of grudge bearing, comes out to watch David and his ragtag entourage. Shimei's rancor erupts and spews, and he starts hurling rocks, dirt, curses down on king and company. One of David's henchmen offers to lop off Shimei's head, but David restrains him: "If he is cursing because the LORD said to him, 'Curse David,' who can ask, 'Why do you do this?' . . . Leave him alone; let him curse, for the LORD has told him to" (2 Sam. 16:10–11).

"So David and his men continued along the road while Shimei was going along the hillside opposite him, cursing as he went and throwing stones at him and showering him with dirt." Then this: "The king and all the people with him arrived at their destination exhausted. And there he refreshed himself" (2 Sam. 16:13–14).

They arrive exhausted. But David refreshes himself—the word in Hebrew is *nephesh.* It is a word related to both breath and soul. Literally, David breathes his soul back to wholeness. He restores the inmost places.

If ever there was a man clearly called, it was David. David stands with Abraham, with Nehemiah, with Paul, with Jesus himself, as one whom God raised up for a great kingdom work. From childhood, David lived with a vivid awareness that God had chosen him to be king over Israel and to be a man after God's own heart. It was a call David relished. It was work because of which he could hardly sleep at night for eagerness to wake and get back to it. It was his food, to do the will of the One who sent him and to finish his work.

But today, with a son usurping him and an old enemy taunting him, he must wonder. Today, his exhaustion must be deeper, and much different, from the tiredness he felt in the old days when he rode in from the battlefield, triumphant again, and hardly had strength left to remove his greaves, pull off his jerkin. That was a good weariness, a weariness full of hope. It was satisfying, teeming already with the seeds of renewal. Those days, he was tired *in* his work. Today, he must be tired *of* it. Today, his exhaustion is of a different order. It is a bleakness. A desolation. A death.

> Men past forty
> Wake at nights,
> Look out at city lights, and wonder:
> Why is life so long,
> And where did I take the wrong turn?[3]

David must be having one of those days that all of us have, even those of us who believe most deeply that what we are doing is what

God sent us to do. A day when we ask, *When did I take the wrong turn? What happened to me? Where did that young man, so alive with faith, so unswerving and unflinching, who never backed off, never second-guessed, never lost heart—where did he go?* David must be having a day when he holds up the work his hands have made and asks, *Is this it? Is this what I bled and wept and strove and lost friends to accomplish? Is this all there is?*

And yet David refreshes himself. He revives his soul.

He takes Sabbath. He finds the rest of God.

And out of that refreshment—breathing in, breathing out—David remembers his first love. David recovers his call. He rises up. He returns to Jerusalem. He defeats his enemies. He resumes his kingship. He leads Israel until his dying day. "And David shepherded them with integrity of heart; / with skillful hands he led them" (Ps. 78:72).

Centuries later, the apostle Peter spoke this epitaph over the king: "For when David *had served God's purpose in his own generation*, he fell asleep" (Acts 13:36, emphasis mine).

Somewhere in there, he got hungry again.

Sabbath Liturgy:
Staying Hungry

In Jesus's parable of the great banquet, it is puzzling why those who first accepted an invitation to the king's feast turned it down the day the meal was actually served. Some of those invited must have lived a stone's throw from the king's palace. All that food—bread baking, meat roasting, confections boiling. The sweetness and spiciness of all those aromas must have mixed and danced like swallows on the air. It must have tantalized the townsfolk for days, made them weak at the knees, light in the head, watery in the mouth. Food prepared is harder to resist than food promised.

But the day of the banquet arrives, and they don't come. Something must have sated them in the meantime.

The story harkens back, in an upside-down way, to Esau's selling his birthright to his brother, Jacob. Esau is so hungry (hungry enough to die, he claims) he trades an irreplaceable heirloom—his status as firstborn, and all the privilege it imparts—for a bowl of stew, a "mess of pottage." Esau throws away treasure for dumplings. In Jesus's story, people do the opposite. They forfeit what is precious by their refusal to come eat. They sell their birthright for an empty bowl.

Both are stories of misplaced hunger. Both are about appetites gone awry. They are about failing to stay hungry for the right things, until the right moment.

In the Bible, food is food—a gift of the earth that makes our bones strong and straight, that lends joy to our gatherings—but it is also a picture of something else: the way God fills and nourishes us. Sometimes our feasting expresses this, and sometimes it eclipses it. Sometimes our abundant meals reflect God's abundance. Other times, all our eating dulls us and lulls us into forgetting him altogether.

In the movie *The Snow Walker*, Charlie Halliday is an arrogant and bigoted pilot who takes a bribe of walrus tusks to transport a sick Inuit girl to Yellowknife. On the way he crashes his plane in a wild expanse of muskeg and tundra. He has few provisions—a case of Coke, a few tins of beans, a can or two of gelatinous ham. But the girl, Kanaalaq, knows how to live off the land: to wait all day to snare a single muskrat, to skewer fish with an improvised harpoon, to set up an elaborate system of decoys to trick caribou into running in circles. Early in their plight, Kanaalaq catches a fish and offers it to Charlie. He pushes it away in disgust. She bites into its raw flesh, and he looks at her with revulsion. "Get out of here. If you want to eat like an animal, go ahead. But don't do it in front of me."

But soon Charlie is starving to death, and Kanaalaq feeds him, at first by her own hands. Initially he is wary, tasting the food she offers with prim caution. But soon he learns to savor it, devour it. In one amazing scene, the two cut strands of raw meat from the thigh of a freshly killed caribou and swallow it down like candy.

It is a tableau of Communion. Charlie has acquired an appetite for *real flesh.* This is no longer about eating out of boredom, craving, or gluttony. He is no longer fussy or squeamish. This is about basic survival.

My food is to do the will of the one who sent me. One thing Jesus did in the Eucharist was to connect, in a vivid and simple way, eating with obedience and worship. He joined earth with heaven, bread with manna, flesh with Spirit. He linked physical hunger with spiritual hunger. He reminded us that every bite is also a prayer.

Do you eat this way? I have two suggestions for this Sabbath Liturgy. The first is that you receive your very next meal—breakfast, lunch, dinner, whatever—as a gift from both heaven and earth. Partake of it with thankfulness and simplicity, eating just enough to fill you, then stopping. Nourish your spirit and your body together. Try to do this whenever you eat and drink.

The other suggestion is that your next Sabbath meal be a feast: a time of enjoying the sheer bounty of God and his creation. Maybe, if you don't do this already, invite others to join you. Overdo it a bit. Delight in the utter extravagance of God, who does exceeding, abundantly more than all we ask or imagine.

In John 21, the risen Christ, repeating an earlier lesson with his disciples, instructs fishermen in their trade. They have fished all night and caught nothing. "Try casting your net on the other side of the boat," Jesus calls to them from the lakeshore. They do, and the nets fill. Peter recognizes that it's Jesus on the beach, and he jumps in and swims to shore. Soon they all arrive, lugging the nets, hauling the fish. Then this: they "saw a fire of burning coals there with fish on it, and some bread" (v. 9).

Jesus always has food we know nothing about.

But he's willing to share.

TWELVE

LISTEN:
Stopping to Hear God

An odd thing happens after you've written a book or two: people start to mistake you for someone who's wise. People from far away, people you've never met—they are sure you have something to say. They have never heard or seen you. You could be tall, shaggy, rumble-voiced, sagacious as Treebeard. You could be squat and jut-boned and leering and devious like Rumpelstiltskin. You might be oily or rusty, grim or comical, poetic or didactic, shy or brash. Your voice could be low and slow and easy on the ears, like Garrison Keillor's, or shrill and breathless and jangly on the nerves, like Edith Bunker's. They don't know if you hold yourself statue-still behind the podium or pace the stage like a man awaiting a life-altering verdict. They know nothing about you, except that you've written a book or two.

They invite you anyhow. They ask you to come, sight unseen, at their expense and speak to crowds of people. It's an amazing feat of trust.

And you go, and everyone is exceptionally generous. A few people are even borderline fawning, astonished, they are, to meet you in the flesh. This feels awkward, and secretly gratifying, like some long-sought vindication over some long-nursed grudge. A few times it's happened that I'm meeting with a group of strangers over a meal and I start to speak, to offer an opinion on some matter or another, and suddenly a vast hush falls over the group. It is the silence of riveted attention, absorbed listening.

It's a wondrous thing. It's like in those movies where some dancer, long mocked or ignored, steps onto the floor, dressed to kill. A ripple of shock goes through the audience. *Is it . . . Umberto? We didn't know he was so darkly handsome, so muscular, so masterful, so powerful.* The music surges, and the guy uncorks. He's a whirling dervish, a Tasmanian devil, a spectacle of athleticism and elegance. All the other dancers stop and move to the edge of the dance floor, clearing the way for him. They watch, at first with envy or scorn, but soon with astonishment. They're spellbound. Except for one person, the dancer's once triumphant and taunting rival. He is mortified. He slinks off, though no one really notices.

That's what this feels like, this moment when people fall silent and listen. *When you have an audience.*

Only I want to stop and tell them they're making a grave error: *I'm a stand-in for the real hero. I'm the custodian, come to sweep the floor for his arrival. Me, I'm stumble-prone. I trip sometimes just walking. I get tangled in my own shoelaces. No, you've mixed me up with someone else. Please, go back to what you were doing.*

But not always. Sometimes I experience something quite the opposite: a sudden expansiveness, a primitive hunger, a craving for more and more and more. *Yes,* I want to say, *now you see. Finally . . .* I'm seized by the urge to grab the microphone, preen in the spotlight, bask in the applause. I want the moment to go on and on.

But afterward, sitting on the edge of my bed in a slightly musty hotel room, or wedged into a narrow seat in the economy coach section of an airplane, with the sleeping stranger beside me tilting precariously my way, I always return to the same thought: *If people stop to listen to you, Mark, to whom are you stopping to listen?*

All our authority is derived. Either God gives us words, or we are only giving opinions. Either God vouches for us, or our credentials are forged. If anyone ever stops to listen to you or me, this had better be solidly in place: *Our speaking comes out of our listening. What we say comes out of what we hear.* We have to be people who listen, day and night, to God. Our utterances ought to be as Jesus's were: an echoing of the Father, an imitation of him. They ought to be a holy ventriloquism, a sacred pantomime. Peter puts it this way: "If anyone speaks, he should do it as one speaking the very words of God" (1 Pet. 4:11). That verse should be paired with Jesus's statement: "He who has ears, let him hear."

But there are so many voices. And there is such little time to listen, to truly listen: to winnow and test it all, to heed and reflect and respond. Carl Sandburg, in his biography of Abraham Lincoln, describes Lincoln's childhood this way: "In wilderness loneliness he companioned with trees, with the faces of open sky and weather in changing seasons, with that individual one-man instrument, the ax. Silence found him for her own. In the making of him, the element of silence was immense."[1]

In the making of him, the element of silence was immense.

What makes me? What makes you? What are the elements that shape us? For certain, there has not been enough silence in my life. Silence is the condition for true listening. But I have too little of it. Silence came visiting and found me already occupied. The element of silence is for me scanty and thin. My existence is a welter of noise.

Henri Nouwen noted that the root of the word *absurd* is the Latin word for "deaf," *surdus.*[2] Absurdness is deafness, where the voice that speaks truth in love, that wounds to heal, that gives clear guidance amidst many false enticements—that voice is lost in the cacophony. We cannot hear it. We are deaf to it. For lack of silence, our lives are absurd. "I confess my sins," poet and farmer Wendell Berry says,

that I have not been happy
enough, considering my good luck;
have listened to too much noise;
have been inattentive to wonders;
have lusted after praise.[3]

I confess my sins: I have done these things also.

When I was a boy, five years old, my father took my brother and me fishing in the Kanaskis, a "wilderness loneliness" of serpentine streams, icy cold, and endless birch forests. The trees there were a lacework of greens in summer, a quiltwork of yellows in fall, a bonework of whites in winter.

It rained almost the entire time. We huddled beneath ponchos glazed dark with rainwater, and my hands were so stiff from cold that I kept having to ask my father to thread my hook with a worm. I can see his face now as he leans close, the beads of rain on his glasses a thousand tiny eyes, each a perfect mirror of that vast, damp grayness all around us.

I remember my dad dousing our sputtering fire with gasoline. The gasoline poured out from the jerry can, hit the smoldering wood, and flared. A rope of fire shot back up into the can's spigot, and the whole thing burst into a fireball. My father stood there a moment juggling it, like a man performing a circus stunt, and then he hurled it all, flame and can, into the river. It gasped and sent up a plume of mauve smoke and white steam. At first he cussed, but afterward he looked sheepish.

I remember my brother and I caught a possum. It played dead so effectively—its body limp and stiff both, its eyes squinted shut—that it fooled us completely, even though our father told us this was its single ploy, its one defense. Even though he told us not to be fooled.

But what I remember most was the silence. *The element of silence was immense.* The second night, the clouds blew off and a fierce, cold moon rose. The stars pressed close and bright as animal eyes at a fire's edge. Falling stars flew like sparks across the sky's blackness. We watched it for a spell, and then we crawled into our small canvas tent. It smelled, from all the wetness, like a root cellar. We lay there and listened. The silence was so vast it had a life all its own. It was not the absence of sound. It was the presence of something very old, very still, very watchful.

We lay like that a long time, in utter stillness, utter quiet. And then a sound pierced the silence. It didn't shatter it: it pierced it, as cleanly as a needle pierces cloth. Even today, nearly forty years on, I hear that sound.

Wolves. Wolves howling. It was the most beautiful, most terrifying sound I've ever known. I wanted it to stop. I wanted it to go on forever. It seemed at once too close and too far. I held my dad and strained my ears to hear, even though the sound was dreadful. Even though it sought me.

In the making of him, the element of silence was immense.

Years passed. I grew, became a man, married, had a son of my own, Adam. When Adam was two, my wife and I took him camping in Oregon, along the coast. We arrived at the campsite early and set up our small tent. Just before evening, the other campsites filled up—mostly with large RVs, "condos on wheels," my wife calls them, long, wide, lumbering monoliths with pull-out canopies and pop-out kitchens and satellite dishes on the roofs.

We bedded early. About ten o'clock at night, a sound awoke us. Many sounds, actually. There had been, earlier, a fragile and tentative silence, but this shattered that. It was a party, just warming up, not to reach its full swing until well after midnight. Country-and-western music rioted from a portable stereo. Several drunken revelers sang along, bellowing in slurred, tuneless voices. Some of the people were crashing into tables and chairs and coolers, square-dancing, I think. So many bottles were clinking it sounded like a wind chime of bones and glass and hubcaps clapping together in a hurricane.

Absurd.

We lay there, sleepless. I thought of Kanaskis and that clear, cold night after hard rain. I thought of lying in a tent about this size. I thought of the silence. I thought of the wolves.

I wondered if they ever come near campgrounds anymore.

And if they do, who's listening?

Samuel had to learn to hear. Samuel was the son of Hannah, God's gift to her after she begged him for a child to end her barrenness. Her barrenness was such sorrow that it made her incoherent, and the priest Eli thought she'd come to the sanctuary drunk. A broken heart can do that. Hannah promised God that if he gave her a son, she would give him back to him. He would be a priest.

God honored her request, and Hannah honored her promise. When Samuel was still a young boy, only just weaned, Hannah took him to the house of the Lord in Shiloh, consecrated him, and left him—though once a year she returned, bearing the gift of a hand-stitched robe, tailored to fit the child's small body.

Samuel "grew up in the presence of the LORD," grew "in stature and in favor with the LORD," and "ministered before the LORD" (1 Sam. 2:21, 26; 3:1). We read all that and then stumble over this: "Now Samuel *did not yet know the LORD*: The word of the LORD had not yet been revealed to him" (3:7, emphasis mine). Thus, with Scripture's classic understatement, we encounter an ancient problem that plagues us still, that is as old as the garden and as contemporary as this morning's news: *we can be very busy for God and still not know him.*

Absurd.

But God means to remedy that, for Samuel and for us. And so one night, God speaks to Samuel. He speaks into the silence in a way that pierces it. In a way that subverts the absurdity. It is a clear voice, unmistakable, inescapable, personal, imperative. It is a voice that demands a response.

"Samuel! Samuel!"

But Samuel thinks it's Eli. Three times he makes this mistake.

Which is understandable. Samuel has been under the tutelage of Eli, apprenticed to Israel's most seasoned priest. Eli would have taught him priestly ways: the rigors of ceremonial washings, the intricacies of food laws, the precise articulation of ritual prayers, the study of Torah. He would have initiated him into all the guild secrets: shown him how to slit the throats of goats and bulls, boil and roast their flesh, carve the fat and the meat of sacrifice. He would have shown him how to mix various concoctions of incense and anointing oil, and which to use for what. Eli would have groomed him well for priesthood.

With one flaw: he didn't teach him to know God. He didn't tutor him in listening to the Voice. He didn't instruct him to know God's word. Amid all that Eli had imparted to Samuel, these things were absent.

Absurd.

Three times God calls Samuel, and three times he mistakes the voice for Eli's. On the third round—by this time, the story is taking on an almost slapstick edge—Eli figures out what's happening. It's the Lord. This is a surprise, the Lord's coming to the house of the Lord. Eli tells Samuel the next time he hears the voice to respond, "Speak, LORD, for your servant is listening" (1 Sam. 3:9).

Samuel lies down. God calls a fourth time. Samuel responds as Eli said. And God speaks, and speaks, and speaks. Thus begins Samuel's intimacy with the Lord. All his finely wrought religious training is transposed into face-to-face encounter. All his theological studies are finally rendered as worship and prayer.

And so: "The LORD was with Samuel as he grew up, and [the Lord] *let none of his words fall to the ground. . . . And Samuel's word came to all Israel*" (1 Sam. 3:19; 4:1, emphasis mine).

The logic of this is straightforward: God protects, preserves, and empowers Samuel's words because Samuel hears, receives, and obeys God's word.

All our authority is derived.
Speak, Lord, for your servant is listening.

What worries me here is myself. I speak a lot, from many platforms. When I'm not speaking, often I'm writing, writing words that have reasonably wide distribution. I'd delight if none of my words fell to the ground—if none were useless, excessive, dispensable, easily dismissed. And I'd delight if my words came to all Israel, all the people of God.

But that's God's business. He might use the means of cyber technology, savvy marketing, good publicity. But either God, God alone, keeps our words from falling and scatters them wide, or else there is nothing in them worth keeping and scattering in the first place. Our concern, our responsibility, is simply to hear and heed God. It is always and everywhere to say, "Speak, Lord, for your servant is listening."

The only authority we have is derived.

There is a rare genetic condition called *synesthesia*—literally, the fusing of sensations. The technical description of synesthesia is "an involuntary physical experience of a cross-modal association"—which means a synesthete's senses are cross-wired by no choice of his own. He experiences sound as color, motion, texture, or smell. The aural—the capacity to hear—is interconnected with the tactile, the kinetic, the visual, the olfactory, so that sound evokes other sensations. The chittering of a bird becomes a pinwheel of light. The nighttime hum of the refrigerator feels like a warm hand pressed lightly on the belly. A child's cry is a window splintering (well, that might be the real thing). The whir of fan blades wafts up like the fragrance of fresh-cut grass. Sound for a synesthete is tangible. It is more "real," more concrete, than for most people. One person out of every twenty-five thousand, according to one estimate, has some form, mild or acute, of synesthesia.[4]

I wonder if there's a spiritual equivalent of that condition, and how many people have it. The apostle John apparently did. "On the

Lord's day," he writes (that is, on the Christian Sabbath), "I was in the Spirit, and I heard behind me a loud voice like a trumpet. . . . I turned around *to see the voice* that was speaking to me" (Rev. 1:10, 12, emphasis mine).

I turned around to see the voice. The voice has an extra weight of tangibility for John. It has such substance, such presence, he doesn't just hear it: he sees it.

He has spiritual synesthesia.

That account contrasts with a Jacob and Esau story in Genesis. Isaac, father of the two brothers, is now old, decrepitly old. And he's blind. He relies on senses other than sight to guide him. The day arrives for Esau to receive his father's blessing—the crowning gift bestowed on Esau in honor of his firstborn status. As part of the blessing ceremony, Esau first goes out to hunt for wild game to bring to his father. But while he's gone, the mother, Rebekah, who favors Jacob, dresses Jacob in Esau's clothing. She covers his hands and neck with animal skins to mimic Esau's hairiness. She helps him prepare a meat dish, just the way Isaac likes it. And she sends Jacob into Isaac's chambers, pretending to be Esau.

He's an orchid thief, this boy, a raider of the lost ark. He's come to steal Esau's greatest treasure: the father's blessing.

Isaac, old, blind Isaac, is suspicious. Something's amiss, he senses. An exchange ensues between father and son.

"Who are you?" he asks.

"Esau," Jacob says, his lie as smooth as his skin.

Isaac expresses surprise at how quickly he's brought back game. Jacob lies again, says God gave him favor in the hunt. Isaac's suspicions are only roused further: "Then Isaac said to Jacob, 'Come near so I can touch you, my son, to know whether you really are my son Esau or not'" (Gen. 27:21). Jacob steps close to his father, who touches him and says, "*The voice is the voice of Jacob, but the hands are the hands of Esau.* . . . Are you really my son Esau?" (27:22, 24, emphasis mine).

Jacob lies again. He says he is Esau.

Isaac lies there in his perpetual night, puzzled and wondering. He leans, I think, upward on his withered arms, juts his face toward a voice he cannot see. Jacob stands there breathless, rigid with fear, wondering as well: *How will this end? What will my father do to me when he forces the truth from me?*

What saves him is an aroma. Jacob brings food to Isaac. He bends to kiss the old man, and his father catches the scent of his clothes. They are Esau's clothes. Isaac smells on them grasslands and forests. He smells dust and smoke and roots, the pungent mix of sweat and wind and blood. He smells, in the weave of the tunic, the insides of wild animals. He catches the aroma of a man who lives by sheer strength and sharpness of instinct. "Ah, the smell of my son / is like the smell of a field / that the LORD has blessed," Isaac declares and blesses him on the spot (Gen. 27:27).

Isaac doesn't trust the voice. He doesn't believe what he hears. He wants further proof and then lets touch and smell trump his sense of hearing. He gives to his other faculties—his nose, his hands—an authority that he denies his ears. If he can feel the thing, sniff the thing, he'll believe it, even against the evidence of the voice.

The voice has little weight compared with everything else. The voice, by his reckoning, is flimsy. It requires further substantiation to verify its authenticity, and other things can quickly overrule it.

Isaac lacks spiritual synesthesia.

I want it. I want God's voice to be to me as it was to John, a thing so real and solid and inescapable I can virtually see it. I want to live by faith, not by sight. And faith comes by hearing. I want to have ears so tuned to the Voice that when God speaks there is no ignoring it.

Speak, Lord, for your servant is listening.

You're wondering what this all has to do with Sabbath. Simply this: we best cultivate the capacity to hear in times of stillness and quietness. *In the making of the man, the element of silence was immense.*

There are two contextual details we know about the apostle John that day he turned to see the Voice. One, he was in exile on Patmos. He was, in other words, under an enforced silence and aloneness, a season of inactivity. Two, it was Sunday, the Lord's Day. It was his Sabbath.[5]

These conditions—the silence, the aloneness, the stillness, the Sabbath—might be beside the point. Then again, they might just be the point. It's possible that they are mentioned because they form the necessary backdrop for true listening. The tent at night in the wilderness, the place where the Voice comes close, becomes clear enough to pierce.

Sabbath is a time to listen. Rabbi Abraham Joshua Heschel claims that Sabbath is a token of eternity, an outpost of heaven. It is time uniquely poised for God's presence. If ever we might expect to *see* a voice, this day ranks highest. A predominant Jewish legend is that God imparted the Torah, the Old Testament law, on the Sabbath: for on this day, the conviction went, Israel listened best, was most attentive to the Voice, and so was least likely to miss the day of God's visitation.[6]

I don't think God is more likely to speak on the Sabbath or the Lord's Day than on any other day. As Paul says, to some one day is sacred, to others all days are alike: what matters is that each is convinced in his own mind (see Rom. 14:5). And Hebrews warns and exhorts, "*Today,* if you hear his voice, / do not harden your hearts" (Heb. 3:7–8, 15; 4:7, emphasis mine). Today is, well, *today.* Right here, right now.

And yet we're called to sanctify Sabbath, literally to betroth it, to think of it as our bride. We're called to take time each week—whether Sunday or another day—and to treat it with an extra measure of reverence, to live in it with a higher degree of attentiveness.

We're called to listen. The book of Hebrews commands us, three times, to listen to the voice that speaks *today.* One of these commands is in the context of Sabbath rest—indeed, the eschatological

Sabbath rest, the Sabbath that fulfills and transcends all others. Hebrews 4—a passage we'll explore more fully in the final chapter—speaks of the Israelites' refusal to fully enter the rest of God. The people under Moses didn't just fail to keep Sabbath; they failed to trust God, *to rest in him*, to believe in the Lord of the Sabbath. They refused to believe that God would protect them and provide for them. For their unbelief—in other words, not for their acts, but for their hard hearts that led to those acts—God punished them by keeping them in the desert forty years. Finally, under Joshua, the next generation of Israel entered the land and entered God's rest.

But the rest wasn't complete. It was only partial. It was preliminary to a greater rest, another Sabbath day God is preparing: "There remains, then, a Sabbath-rest for the people of God" (Heb. 4:9). This day is the reality to which all previous Sabbath days stand as shadows. "Let us, therefore, make every effort to enter that rest" (4:11).

And what effort is required? In a word, to listen, to listen in faith. *Today, if you hear his voice.* The generation under Moses was punished for disobedience and unbelief. But at root, those sins are a failure to hear and heed the Voice of the One who speaks. It is no accident that the lengthy passage in Hebrews about Sabbath rest and hearing God's voice is immediately followed by this:

> For the word of God is living and active. Sharper than any double-edged sword, it penetrates even to dividing soul and spirit, joints and marrow; it judges the thoughts and attitudes of the heart. Nothing in all creation is hidden from God's sight. Everything is uncovered and laid bare before the eyes of him to whom we must give account. (Hebrews 4:12–13)

And that in turn is followed by this:

> Therefore, since we have a great high priest who has gone through the heavens, Jesus the Son of God, let us hold firmly

> to the faith we profess. For we do not have a high priest who is unable to sympathize with our weaknesses, but we have one who has been tempted in every way, just as we are—yet was without sin. Let us then approach the throne of grace with confidence, so that we may receive mercy and find grace to help us in our time of need. (Hebrews 4:14–16)

God is always speaking. "There is no speech or language / where [his] voice is not heard" (Ps. 19:3). But we're not always listening. We don't make the effort and so fail to go boldly into his throne room to receive what we need: a word that can pierce, and cut, and heal.

Here's the paradox: If we don't listen, we never enter his rest. Yet if we don't enter his rest, we never listen.

Practice a deeper listening during Sabbath. Most other days, by necessity as much as by choice, we live amid a clatter of noise. I am a man of unclean lips and live among a people of unclean lips. Certainly, our lips are busy. But Sabbath is when we stop. We slow down. We play, we rest, we dream, we wonder. We cease from that which is necessary and turn to that which gives life. And in the hush that descends, we listen.

Are you listening?

Sabbath Liturgy:
Listening

Deepest truth sometimes hides in plain sight. It reveals itself only to babes and evades the wise and the learned. One hiding place for such truth is children's books, and one of my favorites is Dr. Seuss's *Horton Hears a Who.*

Horton is an elephant whose heart is larger than his brain. But he has enormous ears, and one day he catches, thin and faint, a tiny voice. He traces it to a single spore on the head of a single dandelion gone to seed. On that single spore, so small no eye can behold it, perches an entire world, inhabited by Whos. One Who has come to believe that a world exists outside his own. His cry is an attempt to reach that world beyond.

No one can hear that Who crying, except Horton. He hears, and his heart is broken and ignited by that tiny voice. His life's mission crystallizes: to do all he can, even if it costs him his own life, to rescue the Whos, even if most don't know and don't care. The story's drama unfolds in two parts: the little Whos' nearly vain attempt to convince the other Whos that there is something out there, someone listening, and that survival depends on making contact; and Horton's nearly vain attempt to convince those in his world—especially a band of malicious monkeys—that there is something down there, someone calling, and that they need rescuing.

A preposterous story.

Yet vaguely familiar.

But in some ways, our situation is the exact opposite. With Horton and that little Who, the microscopic world attempts to make contact with the vast world outside. In our case, this is reversed: the larger world, the world of the divine and the eternal, breaks in on our minuscule one, the world of the human and the temporal. "The heavens declare the glory of God," Psalm 19 says. "Day after day they pour forth speech" (vv. 1–2).

But who's listening?

Prayer, before it's talking, ought to be listening. Before it's petition, it should be audition. Before it calls for eloquence, it requires attention. God speaks. We listen. Prayer's best posture is ears cupped, head tilted toward that Voice.

And what does the Voice speak? More often than not, a question. God's curiosity is his most underexplored attribute. He's downright inquisitive, brimful with questions—some childlike blunt, asked in seeming naiveté, others lawyerlike shrewd, asked with stealthy cunning. Many he asks at odd or awkward moments, moments of heightened danger or giddy elation or riveting shame, moments when my impulse—especially were I God—would be to command or announce.

But God asks. He's a God of wonder in more ways than one. Indeed, the very first thing out of God's mouth, after a sustained monologue in which he speaks all creation into existence and declares aloud his pleasure over it, is to ask a question—three, in fact. "Where are you?" "Who told you that you were naked?" "Did you eat from the tree I commanded you not to eat from?"

Does he not know?

I ask questions to discover things. I'm puzzled, so I ask. I'm lost, so I ask (but only when I'm desperately lost, and hopelessly late from being lost, and have just circled the same gas station for the eighth time). I'm incomplete, so I ask. To me, questions are nets for dragging the lake. They're hairpins for picking locks. They're hooks for hauling up deep quarry; they help me get at buried, elusive things. I ask questions because I am vastly ignorant and incurably forgetful, and because the alternative—to live in my ignorance and amnesia—is worse than the trouble of asking.

I ask questions out of my ever-present need and my never-banished folly.

But not God. What does God need or need to know? He lacks nothing: not light, not insight, not knowledge, not power, not love, not the cows on a thousand hills. He has no need for personal growth, anyone's favor, fresh information. He possesses all things in all fullness.

God, strictly speaking, has nothing to ask.

But he asks anyhow. And this, I think, is why: nothing hooks us and pries us open quite like a question. You can talk all day at me, yet it obliges me nothing. I can listen or not, respond or not. But ask me one question, and I must answer or rupture our fellowship. God's inquisitiveness, his seeming curiosity, is a measure of his intimate nature. He desires relationship. He wants to talk *with us*, not just at us, or we at him.

So a key attitude of prayer is listening, and what we listen for most are God's questions. "Where are you?" "Where is your brother?" "Where are the other nine?" "Why do you call me good?" "Why do you call me 'Lord' and not do the things I say?" "Who do you say I am?"

One day, long ago, a blind man named Bartimaeus was sitting at the roadside as Jesus passed by. Bartimaeus heard the commotion—for his ears were good, maybe sharper than most people's—and he cried out to Jesus. He begged for mercy. Many—"those who led the way," according to Luke—told him to shut up. But Jesus has big ears and a big heart. He stopped and had Bartimaeus called to come.

"Cheer up! On your feet!" they told the blind man. *"He's calling you."*

Indeed. And more than calling you: he's asking you too. "What is it," Jesus says, "you want me to do for you?" (See Mark 10:46–52.)

There it is: a whole new world about to be unveiled, just floating up on the smallest spore of a single question.

He who has ears, let him hear.

For this Sabbath Liturgy, find any one of the questions God or

Jesus asks: "Where is your brother?" "Why do you call me good?" "Where are the other nine?" "Who do you say I am?"—there are many.

Choose one.

Ponder it until you hear God asking you the question personally. And then ponder it until you can give an answer.

THIRTEEN

Remember: *Stopping to Pick Up the Pieces*

Calgary, Alberta, sits between the endless flatlands of the prairies—at sunrise, the horizon curves along earth's rim in a wide, smooth line—and the jagged heights of the Rockies—at sunset, their peaks print blue shadows across the city. The geographical combination makes for tempestuous weather: an impossible midwinter cold can break, in the matter of an hour, into a summery balm that turns ice sheets to swamps; or an Arctic front can swoop down on a heat wave in August and close roadways with blizzards. Tornadoes skip and reel across open fields, plucking up heavy things at whim, flinging them loose like confetti. Hailstorms hurl down stones large as fists, flattening crops, dimpling car metal, shredding forests, shattering clapboard. Sometimes rain falls and falls, week on week, until the earth slithers with mud and even tractors wallow and get stuck in it. Other times, the sun blazes and blazes, days without end, until that same earth dries and breaks to potsherds, and the wind scoops it away in clouds of dust.

I was born here. Of all Calgary's fickle weather, what I remember best are the thunderstorms. You could see them gathering all day, over in Saskatchewan or down in Idaho: dense, muscular clouds with a deep, dark purple on their underbellies and an incandescent brightness at their crowns. They were in no hurry, those thunderheads—an army that knew its superior strength, that flaunted it, took its time to assemble in full view, as part of its strategy. By midafternoon, the rumble of the storm's encampment reached us. Bolts of lightning fissured the deepening blackness of those clouds.

By nightfall it was on us: a great fury unleashed, biblical in proportions. The rain usually held off, so the atmosphere was both crackling dry and oppressively humid. The lightning was so close it sizzled the air and left a burnt smell, and right on its heels the thunder crashed, so loud it shook the ground. And the wind: a capricious thing that dropped to a dead calm, eerie still, and then rose up wild and unruly, buffeting cars into ditches, dismembering trees, shearing and unraveling street wires. It needled down chimneys and sluiced through breezeways with a ghoulish shriek.

One evening, as one of these storms began its siege, my parents gathered my brother and me on our front lawn. We all sat together on a blanket, wrapped up together in another one. We watched. My parents were, I'm guessing, oblivious to how dangerous this was: that any one of those lightning bolts, hunting for some upright thing to skewer and char, could easily have picked us, the convenient little bundle of us, and turned us all to a handful of ashes. But that didn't happen, and what I remember is the sheer visceral thrill of being in the midst of that storm, sitting huddled with one another while all that raw power and implacable wildness hurtled about. *Whether it was more like playing with a thunderstorm or playing with a kitten I could never make up my mind.*

I think, because of it, one of my favorite psalms is Psalm 29. Every time I hear it, something leaps in me:

> The voice of the LORD is over the waters;
> the God of glory thunders,
> the LORD thunders over the mighty waters.
> The voice of the LORD is powerful;

the voice of the LORD is majestic.
The voice of the LORD breaks the cedars;
the LORD breaks in pieces the cedars of Lebanon. . . .
The voice of the LORD strikes
with flashes of lightning.
The voice of the LORD shakes the desert. . . .
The voice of the LORD twists the oaks
and strips the forests bare.
And in his temple all cry, "Glory!" (vv. 3–5, 7–9)

Glory, indeed.

I have carried the memory of the night from then until now. I think I will carry it, tucked up high in a place amnesia won't touch, hidden down deep in a cave dementia can't reach, until I die. I have kept that memory as carefully as I have kept other mementos from my youth—my collection of Britains Limited molded figures, tiny replicas of Union and Confederate soldiers, frontier cowboys, medieval knights, that I bought with my allowance piece by piece, week by week, from the cluttered toy shop my mother drove me to every Saturday morning when I was a boy; the agates I gathered in the gravel pit behind our house, walking for hours in a kind of tranced stoop, training my eyes to pick out their amber glint; the photo of me at four years of age, helping my mom and dad whitewash the back porch, a stubby brush capped with paint held aloft in my hand, my mom next to me with a dripping roller, my dad, I suppose, taking the picture. I have passed, several times, the memory of that stormy night to my own children, just as I have passed to my son most of my Britains Limited figures, to my daughters my agates, and one day will pass along that photo, and many more besides.

Memory is identity. Memory grounds us in who we are, where we've come from. Memory shapes us and guides us. "The LORD said to Moses, 'Write this on a scroll *as something to be remembered*, and make sure that Joshua hears it'" (Exod. 17:14, emphasis mine).

Future identity and destiny, in other words, flower from a remembrance of things past.

To remember is, literally, to put broken pieces back together, to *re*-member. It is to create an original wholeness out of what has become scattered fragments. At times it traps us, I know, memory holds us hostage, demands we pay some impossible ransom. But just as often it frees us, reminds us of something we know in our bones but forget in our heads, only to remember it again in the nick of time, before we seal an identity not truly ours.

The movie *The Kid* is about that. It's the story of a man (played by Bruce Willis), a callous and jaded and ruthless man, who makes piles of money spinning people's images. His success depends on his hardness. It depends on his lack of feeling. But, in the alchemy of movies, he meets himself as a chubby, timid, tenderhearted kid. In the exchange, he rediscovers who he really is, who he was meant to be. His childhood self helps his adult self recapture his true identity, and his adult self helps his childhood self become that. The encounter becomes redemptive.

But first he has to remember. He has to piece his broken self back together.

There is a terrible cost to our busyness. It erodes memory. Or worse than that: it turns good memory into mere nostalgia—memory falsified and petrified—and turns bad memory into bloodhounds that chase us to rend us, that keep us ever running, dodging, backtracking. Busyness destroys the time we need to remember well.

In the confusion, we forget who we are. The broken pieces remain strewn.

The Swahili word for "white man"—*mazungu*—literally means "one who spins around." That's how East Africans see Westerners: turning ourselves dizzy, a great whirl of motion without direction. We're flurries of going nowhere.

Sabbath time invites us to stop turning around and around. It invites us, among much else, to remember. And remembering—remembering well, without nostalgia or self-pity or bitterness, but in a way that reminds us of who we are—is the necessary groundwork for reflecting well and anticipating well, the subjects of the next chapter. All these—remembering, reflecting, anticipating—are Sabbath practices.

They are also Eucharistic practices, the ways we approach the bread and the cup of Communion. Jesus told us to eat and drink in remembrance of him, and to do it in anticipation of that day we will eat and drink with him in heaven. He told us, in other words, to look back and to look ahead. The apostle Paul adds one thing to this: when we eat and drink this meal, we ought to examine ourselves and our relationships with others. We ought to look around and look within. We ought to reflect.

Both Sabbath and Eucharist join all three: remember, reflect, anticipate.

This linkage between Sabbath and Communion is not accidental. Eucharist, after all, is the Christian embodiment of the Jewish Passover, and Passover is the High Holy Day of Judaism, the lord of Sabbaths. Just as we approach the Communion table with reverence and awe—we sanctify it and don't treat this as just another meal, another chunk of bread or mouthful of wine—so we ought to approach Sabbath with a sense of its sacredness—that this is not just ordinary time, *chronos* time. This, rather, is *kairos* time, time as sanctuary, time as holy ground.

This is God-given space to remember, reflect, and anticipate.

Let us speak of remembering.

Milan Kundera, the Czech writer, wrote a novel in the seventies called *The Book of Laughter and Forgetting.* Sometimes I think an alternate title for the Bible could be *The Book of Remembering and Forgetting.* A constant scriptural refrain is to remember. Our faith is rooted in memory, so much so that one of the key works of the Holy Spirit is the ministry of reminding (see John 14:26). The day we forget the works of God, from ages past until this very morning, is the day our faith starts to deform into something else—mythology, ideology, superstition, dogmatism, agnosticism, fanaticism. Remembering well is essential to an authentic, living faith.

Equal to this is the capacity to forget. "Forgetting what is behind," Paul writes, "and straining toward what is ahead, I press on toward the goal to win the prize for which God has called me heavenward in Christ Jesus" (Phil. 3:13–14). Only by forgetting, Paul says, can he "press on to take hold of that for which Christ Jesus took hold of me" (3:12). Taking hold of God's call on our lives depends on this quality of forgetfulness. God's future entails a relinquishing of some of our own pasts. God himself wills a holy amnesia in regard to confessed sins: he "will remember their sins no more" (Jer. 31:34).

Certain memories clamor for preeminence but must be denied it. They are bully memories, despotic and spoiled. These are memories—we all know this—that seek to use up all the energy that might otherwise be invested in remembering well, or reflecting truthfully, or anticipating joyfully. This kind of memory is gluttonous, never satisfied with its share. It wants, not just the day it had, but every day, today and tomorrow and tomorrow and tomorrow, until the end of all days.

As a pastor, I've spoken to hundreds of people held hostage by these kinds of memories. Old wounds they keep reopening. Old glories they keep reliving. Old grudges they keep nursing. Old taunts they keep rehearsing. Old fears they keep reviving. Their minds curve back to and curl around these with virtually no provocation. These memories are a prison they've lived in so long they don't know how to live outside it.

They're stuck.

True remembering gets us unstuck.

Do you remember well? "Remember those earlier days after you had received the light, when you stood your ground in a great contest in the face of suffering. . . . Do not throw away your confidence; it will be richly rewarded. You need to persevere" (Heb. 10:32, 35–36).

Do you remember those earlier days? Do you remember the moment you knew you were loved with a love that could not be taken or broken or lost? Do you remember the day the Voice broke into you like a storm, terrifying and healing all at once?

Hold that memory until it's alive, until it assumes its true size and weight and shape. Persevere.

Until it reminds you who you really are.

But our lives consist of more than the abundance of our remembrances. If all we do is remember, the past will not guide us: it will ensnare us. Loss of memory is called *amnesia,* the condition in which life narrows to mere impressions and sensations, without touchstones to interpret them. But the conquest of memory, when memory holds sway over all our thoughts, reduces life to a museum.

The gift of Sabbath is to recollect, yes, but as I've already suggested, it is also to reflect, to pay attention to the present. And it is to project, to nurture expectancy about the future. Those two things, added to memory, allow us to live in the three dimensions of time: then, now, and when. It takes an active, avid participation in all three to be fully human, fully alive, and to fully know the rest of God.

So to reflection and anticipation we turn in the final chapter.

SABBATH LITURGY: Remembering

One of memory's strange mysteries is that we can recall, with vividness, events from a lifetime ago yet forget why we walked into a room. The name of the person standing right in front of you, six inches away, whose hand you just shook—his name slipped you already, didn't it? While the name of the wizened old woman who lived at the end of your street when you were three, whom you saw rarely and talked to never, is as present to you as a stone in your shoe.

There are explanations for all this, explanations that have to do with neurology and developmental theories and other complex things. Even if I knew and grasped all that, even if I could articulate it, I would not do it right now.

I'm thinking about something else. I'm wondering why most of us exercise such poor stewardship over the kingdom of our memories. Why, when memory has such power to make us or ruin us, do we *practice* it so seldom?

One of our first Sabbath Liturgies was paying attention: stopping to notice what is right in front of us. Loss of attentiveness plays into loss of memory. They are blood brothers, we simply don't remember what we never stopped to notice. Some memories, early ones especially, we hold with such tenacity or reject with such ferocity because we couldn't help but pay attention. The memory of the event or person got imprinted on us indelibly through trauma or ecstasy, surprise or revulsion. It burned itself into us, like it or not.

But most won't. This is not an altogether bad thing, to remember everything and everyone would be a disaster, a landslide of image and sensation that would overwhelm us. But neither is it an altogether good thing, for somewhere in that inattention and forgetfulness, we lose that which could ground us and shape us most. If the Israelites ever forgot the Exodus, they forgot who they were. If Christians ever forget Jesus's death and resurrection, we come unhinged from the story that defines us, the story that frames and explains all other stories.

Here is a Sabbath Liturgy borrowed from an ancient Christian practice. It is called the *prayer of examen.* One way to practice this is to review your days at the end of each and to ask two simple questions: *Where did I feel most alive, most hopeful, most in the presence of God? And where did I feel most dead, most despairing, farthest from God?* What fulfilled me, and what left me forsaken? Where did I taste consolation, and where desolation?

This is a good practice all on its own; it trains us in the quirks and rhythms of our hearts and teaches us to track the wind of the Spirit. But it also makes us better stewards of memory. It enshrines those moments, many elusive and capricious, that are probably far more significant in God's eyes than those moments that rivet or command attention. A wild man in camel hair, a young couple in a stable—these are infinitely more significant than all the grandeur and fanfare of Caesar. But they're harder to see. We won't grasp their importance unless we take time to notice.

Try this. At the day's end, crawl into a warm tub or your favorite chair, or maybe—if sleep is not too seductive here—your own bed. Get comfortable. Quiet yourself. Reflect on the day. When were you most alive? What were you doing then, thinking, saying, seeing? When were you most empty? What was going on at that moment?

When did it seem God was close, and when did it seem he was far away?

Practice that each day.

Eventually, you might even remember why you walked into the room.

FOURTEEN

Reflect and Anticipate: *Stopping to Glimpse Forever*

Who are you? We ask that of God. We ask it of others. We ask it of ourselves. It's a question that stands at the heart of the reflective life. Deep calling to deep takes shape around a single inquiry: *Who are you?*

We keep asking, though we never get a full or fully satisfying answer this side of heaven. To think otherwise is to court misery and tragedy. Down here, we only ever see through a glass darkly. We cannot know God or ourselves or anyone else on earth as we will know God and ourselves and everyone else in heaven. We're bleary-eyed from the Fall. In this life we never experience pure and unbroken intimacy with anyone. We never have nakedness without shame. We never have a completely blameless motive. This side of the grave, we never solve the enigma of ourselves and others. Between us, within us, there hangs an opaque wall, blurring and distorting all we look upon.

Who are you?

We're meant to keep asking anyhow, to keep looking all the same, to keep inching toward a shore that appears to retreat with our every advance. *Who are you? Who are you, God, wife, child, friend, self?* To push ever deeper into this mystery, to pry ever further into this discovery, is the ongoing work of reflection.

But reflection flourishes only in rest: stopping long enough to coax out and face things inmost and utmost, things hidden, things lost, things avoided. I knew a man who took two weeks to walk in silence and solitude in the Highlands of Wales. He kept company with stones and fields and cold, starry nights. At first, the journey was a reprieve, a needed break from his life's clutter and scatter. But around the fourth night, something shifted. He grew terribly afraid, but not of wolves, ghosts, brigands, or storms.

He sensed something shadowy and naked stalking him, edging ever closer.

He was afraid of himself.

Solitude unlatched a cellar in him, someplace where memories and longings and fears lay buried, locked up so long he'd almost forgotten them. Aloneness loosed them.

"I thought I'd gone mad," he said. "I felt I couldn't escape. I feared sleeping. I feared waking. I dreaded daytime and nighttime. I wanted to get as far away from myself as I could."

But he had nowhere to hide. After many days, he began to see things he had not seen for years, some for a lifetime. He saw how he avoided closeness with other people, the subtle ways he sabotaged this and made it look as if the other persons were to blame. He saw how he had become busy as a way of eluding his sense of emptiness and insignificance. He saw that all his many accomplishments had never removed from him a primal fear that he was a fraud—and soon to be exposed.

At the end of the two weeks, he knew himself in a way he had never imagined. "It was as if I met myself for the first time. I felt I returned from that two weeks with a soul mate. Or maybe I just returned with a soul."

The story of Jacob in Genesis is, at one level, the story of a man like that, a man always on the run: running from his angry brother, Esau, from his angry father-in-law, Laban. But mostly, running from himself. Jacob is a man with a stolen identity. From the outset, when he grabbed his twin, Esau's, heel in the dark womb and rode out into daylight, he'd been clutching after anything that would complete him, name him, make him, give him an edge. Indeed, that's what his name means: "Heal-grabber." "Trickster." "Taker." "Artful dodger."

Jacob had never really met himself. He took so many things from Esau—Esau's strength in the womb, his birthright, his clothing, his blessing—and took so many things from Laban—two daughters, his best livestock, his household idols—that Jacob forgot who he was. He ensnared himself, then lost himself, in all his conspiracies and double-dealings. He played impostor and trickster to dupe others so often, he duped himself.

The defining moment of Jacob's life—we looked at this scene in an earlier chapter—was when he dressed in Esau's clothes, covered his hands and neck in animal skin to mimic Esau's hairiness, slipped into his blind father, Isaac's, chamber, and stole from him Esau's blessing. Isaac asked Jacob, "Who is it?" And Jacob answered, "I am Esau."

He was lying. But maybe, as well, he really didn't know.

This for sure: it's doubtful Jacob could have answered that question straight under any circumstances. Did he know who he was? Was he able to face it?

But a night comes when Jacob is left alone. In the morning, he must face Esau. The terror of that encounter haunts him. He must be skittish, coiled tight, jumping at every sound coming from the darkness—the owl's hoot, the coyote's cry, the snake's rustle. All seem to him omens. But there is a worse terror to face than Esau, a more frightful encounter afoot.

Something's stalking him.

And then, with cool suddenness, a man steps into the ragged circle of firelight and grabs Jacob's heel. He grabs his wrist, his neck, his arms, so fast, so strong, so agile. Jacob is at first taken off guard. But he's done this before, grappled and hung on for dear life. He's writhed and twisted to win advantage, yes, done it all his life. And so the fight goes on, all through the night's long darkness, until a gray light smolders at the earth's far edge. It is a deadlock, this battle. So the man does violence with a single touch: he maims Jacob, plucks his hip from its socket. And then, pleading for his own sake, pleading for Jacob's, the man says, "Let me go, for it is daybreak" (Gen. 32:26).

Jacob refuses. This is a fight like all the others. This is a fight like none other. This is a fight he cannot afford to lose, and a fight he cannot afford to win. This is a fight that can cripple him and mend him. It can end his exile and make good his homecoming, even if ever after he limps.

But first a question: "The man asked him, 'What is your name?'" (Gen. 32:27).

Who are you?

Jacob can't run, can't hide, can't fight any longer.

"'Jacob,' he answered" (v. 27).

And then a miracle happens, a miracle greater than the reconciliation about to take place between Jacob and Esau, a miracle that perhaps had to happen before that reconciliation was even possible.

Jacob finds out who he really is.

"Your name will no longer be Jacob, but Israel, because you have struggled with God and with men and have overcome" (v. 28).

Jacob then has a request, the same one the man had of him: "Please tell me your name." But the man refuses: "Why do you ask my name?" is all he says (v. 29).

Yet Jacob knows who this is. Somehow—a tone, a gesture, a touch, something—the man discloses his identity. "I saw God face to face," Jacob declares afterward (v. 30).

On that night before meeting Esau, Jacob met himself, really for the first time. And he met God, really for the first time.

I don't think I'm making too much of this story. I have sat more hours than I can tally with people who have avoided themselves so long—often by indulging themselves, by playing Jacob, by coveting what others have and amassing wealth at others' expense—that they have no idea who they are. And almost without exception, these people are going so headlong at life that they have no time, or so they're convinced, and usually no inclination to be alone, to listen, to wait. To reflect. To ask, *Who am I? Who are you?*

I think they're afraid, many of them. They fear the man who stalks them to wrestle them, to wound them, to bless them, to ask them their names, to name them anew.

They fear meeting the men who are really themselves.

They fear meeting the man who is really God.

And, I suppose, more than this, deeper than this, they fear not meeting either.

When are you left alone? When do you step back far enough from all your pressures and possessions, your titles and demands, to truly, deeply reflect?

To meet the man?

I mentioned that I'm writing this book during a sabbatical. In some ways, this sabbatical has become a journey in austere and lonely places. It has been a night encampment by the river Jabbok. It has forced me to be alone with myself often enough that I have tasted a terror greater than meeting wolves, or ghosts, or Esau.

I have had to meet myself. I have had to meet my God. I have had to wrestle the man.

Some of that has been a homecoming. It has been consoling and redemptive. It has allowed me to live more fully in my own skin and to inhabit the world with clarity and honesty. But some of it has been otherwise. It has been a wrenching, bruising encounter that's left me with a limp. God has revealed things about himself that have pierced me. Things I thought I knew but didn't. His holiness, for instance. In my increased quietness and watchfulness, I have glimpsed afresh God's holiness, and it is a quality of harrowing beauty. I am ashamed at the times I have trivialized it. I am grieved at the times I have not stood still to let it scour me clean, sear my lips pure, burn me, and heal me.

And God has revealed things about me—or rather, hammerlocked me and forced me to reveal these things about myself—from which I would rather have kept running. These are things where he can't bless me unless he also wounds me. He can't rename me unless I tell him my real name first, speak it like a confession.

Some of this is deeply personal, and I will keep it that way. But let me share one revelation. I have only now come to see how closely I have tied my sense of self to my abilities. I had no idea how deep this connection was until I stepped back from it. In this time, I have had to understand myself as someone other than pastor, preacher, leader. I have had to relinquish those titles for the time being.

Usually I am so immersed in what I do that I know myself only in relation to it. Who am I? I am pastor to these people. I am the one who opens God's Word for them. I am the one entrusted to lead and to serve them.

And what if all that is taken from me, for a season or forever, by my choosing or in spite of it? I have had now almost three months to ponder that in my heart. I have seen the shape of my own dispensability—a creed I always believed in, but only in the abstract. I now see it in the concrete. The church and the staff thrive in my absence. I occasionally hear of things going on—good things, bad things—and I am powerless to influence any of them. My opinion is not sought. It is not needed.

All this I chose. All this I prayed for. All this I rejoice in.

Still, it startles me. It startles me, not because I thought my colleagues incapable of leading well, but because I thought myself capable of relinquishing leadership well. I thought my identity stood cleanly apart from my gifts. It turns out, me and myself, we're just getting acquainted. Maybe Jacob limped after his encounter with God, not only because God wounded him, but because God pulled from him his crutches, his props, all the external things with which he supported himself. God stripped him of an identity that appeared strong to the world but that was, on the inside, flimsy as moth wings. He clothed him with an identity that looked weak to the world but was strong as an angel's grip.

I'm glad to be shown all this, but a part of me would have rather remained in the dark.

This afternoon, I stood on the sidelines of a muddy field, stood in cold, gray drizzle until the wetness of it soaked my jacket and touched my skin, and watched my son, Adam, play rugby. The brawl of the scrum. The grunts of young men shoving their weight against one another. The almost incandescent cleanness of jerseys getting grass-stained, mud-caked, mired. The ancient instincts of war awakened. My son came off the field bruised, his lip bleeding. He was black with mud, peering out from it like a mummer from his shoe-polish mask, dripping with it like his namesake just plucked from the womb of the earth. He was tired and happy. We got in the van—I covered the seat with an old blanket to keep the mud from the upholstery—and drove home. "Good game," I said, and not much else. We sat together in the sanctuary of that silence, deep calling to deep.

Who am I? I am this man, standing at the edge of that field, sitting in the intimacy of that silence, father to this son.

That's enough.

But that's not all. Both remembering and reflecting bear a certain fruit: anticipating. Anticipation completes the journey that begins with memory and sojourns in reflection. Anticipation is that journey's destination. Apart from this—apart from a nurtured expectancy about things unseen, a growing certainty about things hoped for—some truths about both God and self will remain obscure. Who God really is and who you really are: this is understood, not just in light of the past and the present, but in light of the future too. *Who will you be?* This is as crucial to your full identity as who you have been or have become. The future shapes you as much as the past or the present, maybe more. Destiny, every bit as much as history, determines identity.

We lay hold of this future through anticipation.

Helping people anticipate their future has become my favorite pastoral counseling technique. I am a poor counselor on the best day and mostly have given it up. But not entirely. I used to default to the technique Freud and company bequeathed to the world of therapy. I tried to dredge up the counselee's past, to excavate it in all its rawness and messiness, and then somehow, by some mantra or another, tried to banish the thing. I know dealing with the past is important, and I know many people who are good guides for it. I'm just not in their company. I always seem to botch it. My attempts at it remind me of those old silent horror movies, where the mad scientist creates or awakens something, something green and gooey and fanged, and then loses control of it. The monster wreaks havoc, smashing all the glass things in his lab, terrorizing his assistant, and stalks away in fury to create mayhem *out there.* That was me: awakening what I couldn't placate, spinning disaster from what was supposed to be deliverance.

Then God reoriented me. I sat one day with a young woman who had a desolate past, a blighted landscape of childhood neglect and sexual abuse and, stemming from this, the many broken pieces of her own bad choices. She poured out her story, and I sat speechless. *And now I should say what?* I prayed one of my desperate prayers, "Oh God, Oh God, Oh God!"

And then God slipped me an insight, timely as manna dropped from the sky. He showed me that her past was beyond repair, at least on my watch. If there was any good thing there to salvage, I knew not how. But in the same instant God showed me she still had her future. And it was vast, unbroken, pristine, radiant. It was pure promise: a glory that would be revealed in her, a glory that far outweighed her "light and momentary troubles" now, the glory of the One who was coming to redeem her and transform her (2 Cor. 4:17). Her past was a tragedy to lament. But her future was an epic to anticipate. "Our citizenship is in heaven," Paul says, "and we *eagerly await a Savior from there,* the Lord Jesus Christ, who, by the power that enables him to bring everything under his control, *will transform our lowly bodies so that they will be like his glorious body*" (Phil. 3:20–21, emphasis mine).

Which is simply to say: what *will* happen matters more than what *has* happened.

I shared all this with that young woman, and it became manna to her too. I watched her put on the garment of praise for the spirit of heaviness, the oil of gladness for the ashes of sorrow. I watched her rise and greet the day as it truly was—a day the Lord had made, a day to be glad in, a day to rejoice in, a day new with mercy. And I know the unfolding of this story beyond that day: how that young woman learned to greet each day likewise, how she learned to dig always a little deeper, travel always a little farther, into the hope and the future that were hers through Christ. I know how she met a man, fell in love, married, and had children. And I know how, though some days her past mounted its best attempts to reclaim her for its own, she learned to keep taking hold of her citizenship in heaven, to nurture again and again her eager expectations, and to refuse surrender to anything less.

Since then, this is mostly what I do when I counsel: I help people anticipate. I recognize the value of the other kind of counseling. I just lack skill for it. What I do best is describe, as much as human words allow, the hope to which they have been called, the glory we are to receive. I describe how Jesus has power to bring everything under his control, and how he exerts that control on our behalf, to take us at our lowest and change us into people who resemble him.

This is worth waiting for. This knowledge is our secret treasure, hidden in a place our enemy can't find. But we know where it is. We have the map to it. Maybe now all we hold from it is one small token, a brooch, a coin, a clasp, something so small we can enclose it in a fist. But it is enough to remind us that one day, when we need it most, we inherit all. And then, no matter how wide we spread our arms, it won't be wide enough to hold the overspilling abundance of God's full redemption.

We truly know ourselves only in light of God's future. We truly know God only in the same light. Apart from a compelling vision of things unseen, our lives shrink to things as they are or things as they were. Is the problem you face right now, the family issue or business fiasco or church quarrel or financial dilemma, really as large as you've made it out to be? Seen from the perspective of eternity, does it not scale down to more modest proportions? It's the same with your past. It's easy to let the hurts and slights of yesterday, like an unruly child coloring on the walls, mar all our days. What would happen if instead we let our future loose with a roller and a paint can?

The most determinate fact of reality is not things that were or things that are. It is things to come. It is things that will be:

> Now he has promised, "Once more I will shake not only the earth but also the heavens." The words "once more" indicate the removing of what can be shaken—that is, created things—so that what cannot be shaken may remain.
>
> Therefore, *since we are receiving a kingdom that cannot be shaken*, let us be thankful and so worship God acceptably with reverence and awe, for our "God is a consuming fire." (Hebrews 12:26–29, emphasis mine)

What you see is not what you get. What you see will vanish, never to reappear. What is coming is permanent, never to diminish. It endures forever.

It is more real.

There is only one right and wise response to this, the writer of Hebrews concludes: thanksgiving and worship.

Not complaining or worrying.
Not scheming or tinkering.
Not settling scores or collecting trophies.
Just be thankful and worship.

This is where the book of Hebrews' slant on the Sabbath takes on deep resonance. Hebrews makes explicit the joining of the three dimensions of past, present, and future—then, now, and when—and makes it exactly at this point of Sabbath rest. In Hebrews 3, the writer condemns the generation of Israel under Moses who did not believe God's promise of a land God had prepared for them and so did not enter God's rest.

"Therefore," the writer says in chapter 4, "since the promise of entering his rest still stands, let us be careful that none of you be found to have fallen short of it" (v. 1). Because of their forfeiture, the promise has been extended to you and me. "Now we who have believed enter that rest" (v. 3).

It is a rest both present and future. It is a rest we taste now, enjoy now, receive now. But this present Sabbath is only a shadow of another Sabbath. This other Sabbath is beyond this world. Earthly things suggest it but never fulfill it. Even the rest that God's people received under Joshua, when they entered the Promised Land, was at best a rough facsimile of the rest to come: "For if Joshua had given them rest, God would not have spoken later about another day. There remains, then, a Sabbath-rest for the people of God. . . . Let us, therefore, make every effort to enter that rest" (Heb. 4:8–9, 11).

By faith we make every effort to enter this rest, not by striving, but by trusting. Not by works, but by believing. Later, in Hebrews 11, the writer spells out the nature of this faith: "Faith is being sure of what we hope for and certain of what we do not see" (v. 1).

In that certainty, we live boldly, joyfully, dangerously, dying to self yet fully alive. All of Hebrews 11—the gallery of the faith-filled—shows that. Each of those named in that chapter lived for something that nothing on earth could provide. For all of them, the world was not enough. Only heaven held out that prospect: "By faith [Abraham] made his home in the promised land *like a stranger in a foreign country*; he lived in tents, as did Isaac and Jacob, who were heirs with him of the same promise. For he was looking forward to the city with foundations, whose architect and builder is God" (Heb. 11:9–10, emphasis mine).

Abraham and sons lived like strangers even in the Promised Land. They were vagabonds in paradise, nomads in Shangri-la. They lived that way, not only because God's bequeathing of the land to his people was yet centuries away, but because they knew better anyhow. They knew if they settled in that land, with all its milk and honey and grapes and pomegranates, settled *for* that land, then the true home that was to be the object of their deepest hope would fade from sight. They knew that every inch of the earthly Promised Land, just as every moment of this world's Sabbath rest, was only a foretaste of the true Promised Land and the final Sabbath rest.

Only a foretaste.

Yet still a foretaste. Sabbath isn't eternity, but it's close. It's a kind of precinct of heaven. A well-kept Sabbath is a dress rehearsal for things above. In finding the rest of God now, we prepare for the fullness of God one day.

In Sabbath, we anticipate forever.

Make every effort to enter that.

Sabbath Liturgy: Practicing Heaven

"Faith," the writer of Hebrews says, "is the substance of things hoped for, the evidence of things not seen" (11:1 NKJV). What he has in mind is, not any earthly hope, but a heavenly one—a city whose architect and builder is God. There Jesus is seated at the right hand of God, cheering and coaxing us on. Faith is clarity about that. It is a tenacious conviction that this world is not enough and was never intended to be. It is a steadfast refusal to seek ultimate things—ultimate pleasure, ultimate fulfillment, ultimate purpose, ultimate understanding—where God has not laid them. Not one ultimate thing is stored down here. God has kept them for our homecoming, and none can be filched beforehand.

The eclipse of heaven,[1] as one writer calls it, is a massive loss to the contemporary Western church. We have become so earthly minded we're of little heavenly good—or earthly good, for that matter. In fact, the current malaise in the church, the weariness and jadedness we see all over, is I think largely due to this. We have let consumerism tutor the church in its creed of more, better, brighter, faster. So we have fostered expectations that no church, no home group, no pulpit, no band of brothers, no brand of worship, no conference, no Bible school can ever deliver. The shortfall between what we dream and what we get is vast. All is weighed and found wanting in our sight.

Only we set our sights on the wrong horizon.

The truth is, we're always a bit restless. We're supposed to be. This is not a flaw in our faith, it is faith's substance. It is a divine ruse to keep us from making permanent settlement this side of eternity. Our citizenship is in heaven. Between now and then, here and there, we live as sojourners, Bedouins, exiles, tent dwellers. There is always a little sand in the sheets. There is always a sense that *over there* is better than right here. If ever we achieved perfect Sabbath here, unbroken rest and restfulness, then the eternal rest that Sabbath hints at would become irrelevant.

God lets us groan now to woo us heavenward. He gives us rest here, but not enough to fully satisfy, just enough to keep us in the race. With rest he mixes restlessness. Vacations are always too short, always less than ideal. Dream homes have problems, some nightmarish—leaky pipes, creaky joists, faulty wires, cracking foundations. Good health is hard to maintain and snatched at the whim of some rogue gene or sudden mishap or stray virus. Community is fragile, and even amid close friends we feel a little lonely.

Sabbath is for rest. But it is also a good opportunity to point our restlessness heavenward. Like a wisteria plant, our restlessness needs to be trained to go in a certain direction, or else it follows a path of least resistance. When we recognize that our loneliness, our hunger, our weariness, our disappointment—that these are not final verdicts but only rumors of things unseen, it changes their meaning. It empties them of their power to defeat us. It fills them with an energy to spur us toward deeper hope.

Jesus, speaking of things unseen, often talked about "how much more." If you, though evil, know how to give good gifts, *how much more* does your Father in heaven? If even bad judges eventually dispense justice, *how much more* our God?

This last Sabbath Liturgy is to help train your restless heart heavenward, and it borrows from the logic of "how much more." If this meal with friends and family is rich, *how much more* the banquet of the great King? If resting in this patch of sunlight is refreshing, *how much more* to rest in that place where God and the Lamb shine brighter than any sun? If lovemaking with my spouse is blissful, *how much more* what no eye has seen and no ear heard but which God prepares for those he loves?

Take anything you delight in here on earth: Your children. Your craftwork. Your hot tub. The dewed green of a fairway on a July morning. The sweet corn from your garden, butter-drenched.

Enjoy them all. Find rest in them.

But imagine *how much more* awaits you.

EPILOGUE

Now Stop

In 1976, archaeologist Mary Leakey, rooting and sifting for bones and relics on the plains of Tanzania, made a groundbreaking discovery: a single footprint in what was once damp volcanic ash. There it was, the hard ball of the heel, the light arch of the instep, the plump curve of the big toe, stamped as perfectly as an orthopedist's plaster cast. She set out to uncover what else might be buried there and dug up a length of human footprints, a pair of them like a rough basting stitch in the earth. There were fifty-four in all. These came to be called the Laetoli Footprints. They marked the brief journey of two long-ago companions, both short and with quick, brusque strides, keeping step for step. They walked for a spell, stopped, turned slightly to glance behind them, then carried on.

Who knows who they were: a man and his wife, perhaps, walking uneasily beneath the volcano's smoking shadow, or a father and his son hunting under a brooding sky, or two women seeking water. Who knows? The Laetoli Footprints give us an intriguing, elusive glimpse into a moment of history eons old.

For three years, Mary Leakey's team studied, measured, analyzed, photographed, and took casts of the footprints. And then, finished, they buried them again, to protect them from damage, both natural and human. But here they made a mistake: the materials they used to cover the tracks were riddled with the seeds of acacia trees. Some sprouted, and their roots twined down into the brittle volcanic earth, playing havoc with the footprints. In 1995, the site was reexcavated, the tree roots unraveled and plucked out. But what to do now? Someone proposed carving up the printed rock into massive slabs, crating them, shipping them, storing them in a museum warehouse. This plan was rejected for being too complicated and costly, too likely to go awry. Someone else suggested building a museum of sorts over the footprints, a kind of private vault for them. This was rejected for being too difficult to maintain in such a remote area.

So they buried them again. This time they started with a layer of fine sand, minutely sieved to winnow out all hint of seed. Over this they laid a thick coating of porous plastic, to let rainwater through but nothing that germinated. And then more sand. And then root-defying textiles, and more sand, and more tiles. They crowned it all with soil and lava boulders.[1]

And so they lie there today in northern Tanzania, the Laetoli Footprints, hidden deep beneath tons of earth and things of man's devising, twice buried. It's funny, when you think about it. Those two people, whoever they were, could never have imagined their day's journey—the sooty ground, the burning sky—would one day cause an international stir: that it would take herculean effort and Solomonic wisdom and Crossian wealth to simply uncover and cover the remnants of their ancient stroll.

And funnier still that the only way we can figure out how to keep something is to bury it.

How many times in history—and maybe personally—have we uncovered Sabbath, only to find it is too fragile a thing to preserve in the open air, and so buried it again? I fear that in writing this book. I have done the best I know how to excavate the gift of Sabbath in its original form, to measure the depth and shape and length of its imprint. But I fear it won't take long for erosion to set in, and then for us to spread layers and layers of fill over it. We'll do this first to protect it, but in essence we'll conceal it and then in time forget it.

Jesus's Sabbath-keeping always looked, to his enemies, like Sabbath-breaking. That was one of the many ironies of their accusations against him: people who knew nothing of rest accused a man whose every word and gesture came from rest of Sabbath-breaking. Nevertheless, they hurled their accusations. There he was, Jesus, cutting across a farmer's field and plucking new grain as he went, each seed like a slender, petrified tear. He cupped handfuls of it in the wideness of his carpenter's palm and offered some to his disciples. To his opponents, he appeared to flagrantly violate all they believed most sacred about Sabbath-keeping. To Jesus, he was simply fulfilling the day's true intent. His were acts that sacralized the day, kept it holy. His gestures enshrined the day as a gift bestowed on us, shaped into a gift to give back to God. To Jesus, these were the means by which Sabbath is preserved, held pristine, protected from both erosion and encrustation.

"The Sabbath," Jesus said, "was made for man, not man for the Sabbath" (Mark 2:27).

And that, actually, is all we need to know to keep the Sabbath holy. This day was made for us. God gave it to you and me for our sake, for our benefit, for our strengthening and our replenishment. That is the point religion always forgets, not just about Sabbath, but about virtually everything. Religion is insidiously idolatrous, taking good things and giving them a centrality and veneration out of proportion to the thing itself. Religion makes fetishes of mere tools, icons of sheer gifts. It hallows the form and profanes the substance.

Religion did that with the Sabbath in Jesus's day. What was meant to serve people ended up demanding tribute from them. What was meant to restore people was turned into their drudgery. What was meant to be gift became a kind of punishment. What was intended to be our handmaiden became our despot. We found ourselves spending so much energy just trying to keep this thing from eroding, so much time fussing over it.

So we buried it, buried it deep, and forgot it.

And now we're all tired. Now we dream of that day when our work will be done, when we can finally wash the dust of it from our skin, but that day never comes. We look in vain for the day of our work's completion. But it is mythical, like unicorns and dragons. So we dream, instead, of evacuating our lives, of somehow taking leave of our duties and responsibilities, for a month, or three months, or a year, or more.

But what about Sabbath? Sabbath was made for man. It was something God prepared long ago, inscribed into the very order of creation: a day when all the other days loosed their grip. They were forced to. It's a day that God intended to *fuss over us*, not we over it. It was designed to protect us, pay tribute to us, coddle us, in all our created frailty and God-imprinted beauty and hard-won liberty, in our status as men and women whom God made in his own image and freed by his own hand and own blood.

It is a father's gift to indulge his children.

Before we ever keep the Sabbath holy, it keeps us holy. All we do is tend that which tends us. We feather the bed we sleep on. We feed the goose that lays the golden eggs. God, out of the bounty of his own nature, held this day apart and stepped fully into it, then turned and said, "Come, all you who are weary and heavy-laden. Come, and I will give you rest. Come, join me here."

He makes the footprints, and we just follow along beside.

In one of my other books, I tell the story about the time Philipp Melanchthon turned to Martin Luther and announced, "Today, you and I shall discuss the governance of the universe." Luther looked at Melanchthon and said, "No. Today, you and I shall go fishing and leave the governance of the universe to God."

Ah, the rest of God.

NOTES

INTRODUCTION

1. Mary Oliver, "The Swan," *New & Selected Poems,* Vol. 1 (Boston: Beacon Press, 1992), 79.

CHAPTER 1

1. Scott Adams, *The Dilbert Principle: A Cubicle's-Eye View of Bosses, Meetings, Management Fads & Other Workplace Afflictions* (New York: Collins, 1997); cited in *Leadership Journal: A Practical Journal for Church Leaders,* Fall 1997, 81.
2. Source unknown.
3. Studs Terkel, *Working: People Talk About What They Do All Day and How They Feel About What They Do,* (New York: New Press, 1997).
4. Abraham Joshua Heschel, *The Sabbath* (New York: Farrar, Straus, & Giroux, 2001), 47.
5. Os Guinness, *The Call: Finding and Fulfilling the Central Purpose of Your Life* (Nashville: W Publishing, 1998), 194–95.

CHAPTER 2

1. Leaving mother and father was part of God's original charge to Adam—oddly, since he had neither. But the idea is so central to what God wants to communicate to men and women about marriage that Adam, the first man, was told to do it anyway.
2. Witold Rybczynski, *Waiting for the Weekend* (New York: Penquin, 1991), 13–14.
3. I first heard this from Gary Collins, a former British Columbia Finance Minister and a pilot. I have since confirmed it with several pilots.

CHAPTER 3

1. Wayne Muller, *Sabbath: Restoring the Sacred Rhythm of Rest* (New York: Bantam, 1999), 3.
2. Ibid, 2.
3. Ibid, 4.
4. From *The Cat in the Hat* By Dr. Seuss, copyright TM & copyright by Dr. Seuss Enterprises L. P., 1970, renewed 1998. Used by permission of Random House Children's Books, a division of Random House, Inc.
5. Eugene Peterson, *Eat This Book: The Holy Community at Table with Holy Scripture* (Vancouver, BC: Regent College Publishing, 2000), 43.
6. Unpublished poem by Loni Searl, 2004. Used by permission. All rights reserved.

CHAPTER 4

1. Sietze Buning (Stanley Wiersma), "Obedience" found in *Purpaleanie and Other Permutations* (Orange City, IA: Middleburg Press, 1978). Used with permission of the Middleburg Press, Box 166, Orange City, IA 51041.
2. C. S. Lewis, *Prince Caspian* (England: Puffin Books, 1978), 123–24.

CHAPTER 5

1. Henri J. M. Nouwen, *Reaching Out* (New York: Bantam, 1986).
2. Mary Oliver, "Entering the Kingdom," *New & Used Selected Poems*, Vol. 1 (Boston: Beacon Press, 1992), 190.
3. Ralph Schoenstein, "The Great T. P. Shortage," *TV Guide* (New York: TV Guide, 1974).

CHAPTER 6

1. Christopher de Vinck, *The Power of the Powerless* (Grand Rapids: Zondervan, 1988). Used by permission.

CHAPTER 7

1. Rob Stitch, Tom Gleisner, and Santo Cilario, *Molvania: A Land Untouched by Modern Dentistry* (London: Atlantic Books, 2004), 74.

2. John Ortberg, "Spiritual Disciplines for Leaders," CCN Broadcast, June 15, 2004.
3. From *MR. BROWN CAN MOO! CAN YOU?* by Dr. Seuss, copyright TM & copyright by Dr. Seuss Enterprises L. P., 1970, renewed 1998. Used by permission of Random House Children's Books, a division of Random House, Inc.

CHAPTER 8

1. John Calvin via Dr. Klaus Bockmuehl's 1988 Regent College Lectures on the Decalogue.
2. Excerpt from *The Fellowship of the Ring* by J.R.R. Tolkien. Copyright ©1954, 1965 by J. R. R. Tolkien. Copyright © renewed 1982 by Christopher R. Tolkien, Michael H. R. Tolkien, John F. R. Tolkien, and Priscilla M. A. R. Tolkien. Copyright © renewed 1993 by Christopher R. Tolkien, Michael H. R. Tolkien, John F. R. Tolkien, and Priscilla M. A. R. Tolkien. Reprinted by permission of Houghton Mifflin Company. All rights reserved. (Thank you to my good friend and brother-in-arms, Greg Charyna, for drawing my attention to this passage.)
3. Lauren Winner, *Mudhouse Sabbath* (Brewster, MA: Paraclete, 2003).

CHAPTER 9

1. C. S. Lewis, *The Lion, The Witch, and The Wardrobe* (London: Puffin Books, 1978), 148–49.
2. Abraham Joshua Heschel, *The Sabbath* (New York: Farrar, Straus, & Giroux, 2001), 74.

CHAPTER 10

1. Nell Boyce, "In a Hurry to Slow Life's Clock," *U.S. News & World Report,* January 29, 2003, 74–5.

CHAPTER 11

1. Dorothy Bass, *Receiving the Day: Christian Practices for Opening the Gift of Time* (San Francisco: Jossey-Bass, 2000), 105.

2. Thomas B. Costain, *The Three Edwards* (New York: Buccaneer Books, 1994).
3. Ed Sissman, cited in Gordon McDonald, *The Life God Blesses: Weathering the Storms of Life that Threaten the Soul* (Nashville: Thomas Nelson, 1994), 114.

CHAPTER 12

1. Carl Sandburg, *Abraham Lincoln: The Prairie Years and the War Years* (New York: Harcourt, 1954), 15.
2. Wayne Muller, *Sabbath: Restoring the Sacred Rhythm of Rest* (New York: Bantam, 1999), 84.
3. Wendell Berry, "A Purification," cited in Dorothy Bass, *Receiving the Day: Christian Practices for Opening the Gift of Time* (San Francisco: Jossey-Bass, 2000), 93–4.
4. See the popular website on synesthesia—http://www.macalester.edu/~psych/whathap/UBNRP/synesthsia/intro.html
5. The early church changed Sabbath observance from Saturday, the Jewish Sabbath, to Sunday, the Lord's Day, as a commemoration of Christ's Sunday morning resurrection.
6. Abraham Joshua Heschel, *The Sabbath* (New York: Farrar, Straus, & Giroux, 2001), 74, 83.

CHAPTER 14

1. A. J. Conyers, *The Eclipse of Heaven: The Loss of Transcendence and Its Effect on Modern Life.* (Chicago: St. Augustine's Press, 1999).

EPILOGUE

1. David Wells, "Preservation of the Laetoli Footprints," *Airlines: Canada's Premier Airport Magazine*, July 2004, 67.